new crewel
THE MOTIF COLLECTION

new crewel
THE MOTIF COLLECTION
more exquisite designs in modern embroidery

KATHERINE SHAUGHNESSY

LARK CRAFTS
Asheville

Editor:
Valerie Van Arsdale Shrader
Art Director:
Megan Kirby
Illustrator:
Orrin Lundgren
Photographers:
Lynne Harty
Steve Mann
Cover Designer:
Amy Sly

An Imprint of Sterling Publishing
387 Park Avenue South
New York, NY 10016

If you have questions or comments about
this book, please visit: larkcrafts.com

Library of Congress Cataloging-in-Publication Data

Shaughnessy, Katherine, 1970-
   New crewel : the motif collection : more exquisite designs in modern embroidery / Katherine Shaughnessy. — 1st ed.
      p. cm.
   Includes index.
   ISBN 978-1-60059-795-4
   1. Crewelwork--Patterns. I. Title.
   TT778.C7S532 2012
   746.44'6--dc23

                                                        2011031992

10 9 8 7 6 5 4 3 2 1

First Edition

Published by Lark Crafts,
An Imprint of Sterling Publishing Co., Inc.,
387 Park Avenue South, New York, NY 10016

Text © 2012, Katherine Shaughnessy
Photography © 2012, Lark Crafts, an Imprint of Sterling Publishing Co., Inc., unless otherwise specified
Illustrations © 2012, Lark Crafts, an Imprint of Sterling Publishing Co., Inc., unless otherwise specified

Distributed in Canada by Sterling Publishing, c/o Canadian Manda Group, 165 Dufferin Street, Toronto, Ontario,
Canada M6K 3H6

Distributed in the United Kingdom by GMC Distribution Services, Castle Place, 166 High Street, Lewes, East Sussex,
England BN7 1XU

Distributed in Australia by Capricorn Link (Australia) Pty Ltd., P.O. Box 704, Windsor, NSW 2756 Australia

Manufactured in China

ISBN 13: 978-1-60059-795-4

For information about custom editions, special sales, and premium and corporate purchases, please contact Sterling
Special Sales Department at 800-805-5489 or specialsales@sterlingpub.com.

Requests for information about desk and examination copies available to college and university professors must be
submitted to academic@larkbooks.com. Our complete policy can be found at www.larkcrafts.com.

CONTENTS

This book is dedicated to author and embroiderer
Erica Wilson (October 8, 1928–December 13, 2011).

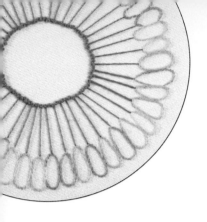

INTRODUCTION

Putting a contemporary spin on the ancient craft of crewelwork, *New Crewel: The Motif Collection* is filled with ideas that will delight and inspire embroiderers of all skill levels. Whether you're a seasoned stitcher searching for innovative crewel projects or a curious beginner eager to learn the basics, you'll find what you're looking for on the pages that follow.

In my first book, *The New Crewel: Exquisite Designs in Contemporary Embroidery* (Lark Crafts, 2005), I introduced a modern approach to crewel without altering the materials and tools traditionally used in crewel embroidery. The positive response to the book was overwhelming. In addition to serving as a source of creative inspiration, *The New Crewel* turned out to be a very useful teaching tool for myself and other experienced embroiderers. The book has accompanied me to crewel classes all over the country. I hope that the fresh designs, new projects, and variety of stitches offered in this book make it an equally helpful instructional aid for crewel teachers and students alike.

If you're new to the craft, here's a bit of background: Crewelwork is a form of embroidery that uses two-ply worsted wool threads on linen fabric. Contrary to popular belief, what separates crewelwork from other forms of embroidery is not the stitches but the use of wool thread on linen fabric. That's it. Other types of embroidery may use silk or cotton threads on a myriad of fabrics, but crewel is just wool on linen. Keep that fact in mind, and any of the hundreds of embroidery stitches out there become fair game. Try them all!

The roots of crewel can be traced back to 17th-century England. The Jacobean crewelwork of that era, with its scenes of swirling flora and fauna stitched in deep greens, warm browns, and variegated reds, is the most recognizable style from that time. After fading in and out of popularity during the subsequent centuries, crewel experienced a major rebirth in the 1960s, with more Jacobean-influenced designs, as well as a flood of kitschy owls, mushrooms, and daisies stitched on colored linen.

I'm excited by the fact that another crewel movement seems to be taking place. During the past eight years, I've watched interest in crewel grow on craft blogs and websites. I've witnessed growth firsthand at weekly craft nights in Marfa, Texas, where I live, and seen evidence of it on the walls of big-city art galleries. Without a doubt, crafters and artists around the world are using the richness of embroidery to create new textile designs and cutting-edge contemporary art.

My new motifs and color palette were inspired by patterns found in nature and by the whimsical artwork of my four-year-old son and five-year-old daughter. Created specifically for this book, the 30 new designs are featured in a special gallery section. To help you get started, I've included a brief basics chapter with information on materials, tools, and techniques, as well as an overview of my favorite stitches. Many of these have been around forever, but a few, like the Circular Couching Stitch and the Circular Filling Stitch, I invented inadvertently, through basic trial and error. Once

you get the hang of them, you'll be ready to tackle the motifs and explore the 8 simple projects that round out the book.

If you're experimentally—or digitally—inclined, the enclosed CD is a fun way to play around with the motifs. You can use the disc to resize and print out the patterns. The possibilities are endless!

As an artist, my goal is to create engaging images with an emphasis on color and texture. I believe that less is more, so most of my motifs require only two or three stitches and four or five different colors of thread. If you're someone who prefers "more," know that any of the designs in this book can be enlarged, made smaller, and/or repeated, creating patterns that go on and on. You can also use my designs as jumping-off points for your own New Crewel explorations. Whatever direction you choose, I hope you'll be as rewarded and enriched as I have been by this long-lasting craft.

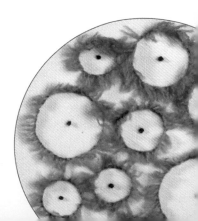

NEW CREWEL
BASICS

MATERIALS

You'll need to gather a number of basic supplies in order complete the motifs and projects in this book. This section describes the materials you can find in craft and needlework stores.

LINEN TWILL

Linen twill is the traditional fabric base for crewelwork. It's a very sturdy, natural material. When woven in a twill pattern, linen doesn't have the grid-like system of holes seen in the plain-weave fabrics of needlepoint and cross-stitch (**figure 1**). The tight, smooth, uninterrupted surface of a twill weave is perfect for the freeform style of crewel embroidery you'll be undertaking (**figure 2**).

Many needlecraft shops and online stores specializing in embroidery supplies carry linen twills specifically for crewelwork in either 100 percent linen or a linen blend. Most linen twills come in white or off-white but can be easily colored before you embroider them using a fabric dye from a craft store or drugstore. All of the designs in this book were done on white linen twill found at an embroidery supply shop.

Although linen twill is the traditional fabric for crewelwork, I can't help breaking the rules! Some of the projects in this book feature materials other than linen, including felted wool, linen plain weave, and aluminum screening. No matter what materials you use, keep in mind that the wool thread you'll be stitching with tends to shrink. Therefore, your projects—whether done on linen twill or polyester fleece—must either be dry-cleaned or carefully hand washed in cold water and air-dried.

Plain Weave

①

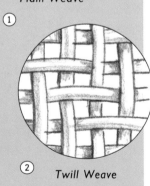

② *Twill Weave*

CREWEL WOOL THREAD

The thread—or yarn—used in crewel embroidery is loosely twisted two-ply worsted wool. Worsted wool isn't soft and fuzzy like knitting yarn. It comes from longhaired English sheep and is combed and spun until it's smooth like a rope. Two strands of this worsted wool are loosely twisted together to make two-ply crewel wool thread (**figure 3**).

Most needlecraft shops and online stores carry several brands of crewel wool thread. Hundreds of colors are available, allowing for both dramatic and subtle color changes, similar to a painter's palette. Crewel wool is sold by the hank, a fairly large quantity, or by the skein, a smaller quantity. To make the projects in this book, you should buy your wool in skeins.

Because crewel wool thread is not very strong, you should use pieces of thread no more than 14 inches (35.5 cm) long when doing crewelwork. You should begin a new piece of thread as soon as the one you're working with starts to wear out.

Tapestry wool thread, used for needlepoint, is made through the same process as crewel wool but is heavier and comes in two, three, and four dividable strands.

③
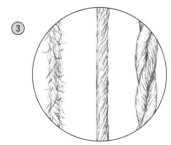

*Knitting Yarn, Worsted Wool,
Two-Ply Worsted*

EMBROIDERY HOOPS

To make your surface smooth as you embroider, your fabric should be held taut. Embroidery hoops do just that; the fabric is sandwiched between two nested rings that are screwed snugly together so that the fabric is tight, like a drum.

Hoops come in different shapes and sizes. They are round, oval, or square, and made of wood, plastic, or metal. A simple, round, unfinished wood hoop that you'll find at most craft stores will get you started. All of the patterns and projects in this book can easily be done using a round hoop, 6 inches (15.3 cm) in diameter. If crewelwork becomes your thing, you may want to invest in several different sizes of the smooth hardwood hoops sold at needlecraft stores or online shops that carry tools for needlepoint, crewel, and cross-stitch.

In addition to hoops, adjustable wooden slat frames and upholstered wood pin frames can be used to hold embroidery fabric taut. These frame types are square or rectangular and are very useful for large crewelwork projects.

THREAD RING OR THREAD CARD

If crewelwork becomes an obsession for you, you may want to make a thread card or find a wooden ring to keep your threads organized, as Jane Rainbow suggests in her book *Beginner's Guide to Crewel Embroidery* (Search Press, 1999). For both the ring and the card, you'll need to cut your threads into 14-inch (35.5 cm) lengths. To do this, unwind an entire skein onto a book that's 7 inches (17.7 cm) wide. Then slide the wound threads off and cut the whole bunch in half (**figure 4**).

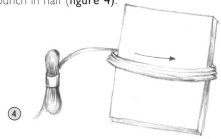

For the thread ring, you'll need a wooden ring similar to the inside ring of an embroidery hoop. Fold a handful of the 14-inch (35.5 cm) lengths in half. Loop the folded threads around the ring, pulling the cut ends to tighten the loop (**figure 5**). Continue adding all of your threads in numerical order. Keep an index card nearby with the list of colors and numbers so you can keep track. Now you can easily pull a single length of thread from the looped area while the rest of the threads stay in place (**figure 6**). Nice!

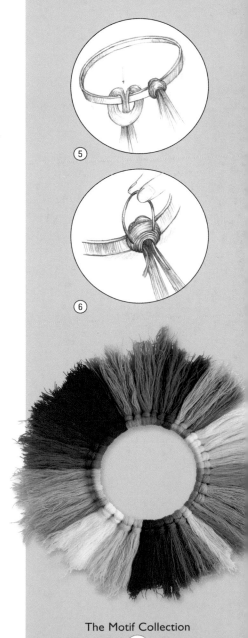

For the thread card, you'll need a piece of card-stock and a hole-punch. Punch a series of holes at least 2 inches (5 cm) apart and about ½ inch (1.25 cm) from one edge of the cardstock. Fold a handful of cut lengths of crewel wool thread in half and thread the folded end into one of the holes, entering from the front of the card. A loop will form. Then, grasping the cut ends, slide them into the loop and pull until the loop is snug on the card. Write the corresponding name, color number, and brand name next to each loop. If you like, punch three holes along the opposite edge of the card and store it in a three-ring binder. As your collection grows, you can add cards to your binder.

NEEDLES

For crewel embroidery, you can use either a crewel needle or a chenille needle. Unlike tapestry needles, which are commonly used for needlepoint and cross-stitch, chenille and crewel needles have very sharp points. The crewel needle is longer, with a short eye. The chenille needle is shorter, with a long eye. When working on tightly woven linen twill, I recommend that you use either a size 3, 4, 5, or 6 crewel needle or a size 20, 22, or 24 chenille needle (the bigger the number, the smaller the needle). Most of the crewelwork in this book was done using a size 24 chenille needle.

The right needle size depends on both your own comfort and the fabric you're using. For easier threading and for beginners, it might be better to begin with a larger needle (i.e., a size 20 chenille or a size 3 crewel). But, given that the needle's key function is to guide the thread back and forth through the fabric, it's important to pick one that's neither too big nor too small. The correct size needle will make a temporary hole in the linen fabric for the thread to easily pass through. If your needle is too small, the thread will quickly wear out as it's dragged

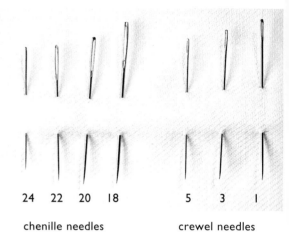

24   22   20   18   5   3   1

chenille needles   crewel needles

through the tight fabric on each pass. And if your needle is too large, it may create unnecessary work for you as you push it through the fabric each time, and it may distort the fabric so much that the temporary holes don't disappear after stitching. By the way, as hard as it is to imagine, too much embroidery can be … um, cruel. Not only do fingers wear out, but needles do, too. When the point of your needle starts to dull, pick a new one.

When your embroidery is finished, you may want to stitch it into something else, like a pillow or an eyeglass case. For many of the projects in this book that needed additional stitching, I hand stitched them using hand-quilter's thread and a hand-sewing needle called a betweens needle. You can use any good quality sewing thread and a sharp or a darner needle as well. Betweens, sharps, and darners are the most common needles found in Grandma's sewing box. They vary in size and length, but all have fairly small eyes. Choose the needle that works best for you.

TOOLS

If you're a home sewer, you probably have most of these tools on hand.

SCISSORS

While one little pair of embroidery scissors will suffice for snipping your crewelwork threads, you'll need a larger pair of fabric scissors capable of cutting your linen twill. In addition, it's nice to have a pair of pinking shears. Cutting fabric with pinking shears helps to prevent the fabric from fraying while you work.

TRACING PAPER

To transfer the designs in this book (or designs of your own), you'll need paper for tracing the design, a fabric pen or pencil, and a light source. It's best to get traditional translucent tracing paper, which you can find at craft and art-supply stores, but regular white copy paper works well in a pinch.

FABRIC PEN

Fabric pens are available at most fabric stores. The ink is usually blue or purple. I like both the water-erasable pens, which disappear with the slightest contact with water, and the air-vanishing pens that fade over time. Before you outline your design, test the fabric pen on a small corner of your fabric to be sure the ink really does disappear.

LIGHT TABLE OR SUNNY WINDOW

You'll need either a light table or a sunny window to backlight your design so that you can trace it onto the fabric.

ESSENTIAL SUPPLIES

You'll need the following basic household items for preparing your fabric before you trace a design, and for pressing your finished crewelwork: an iron, an ironing board, a spray bottle, a lightweight cotton cloth, and a terrycloth towel. If your linen fabric is wrinkled, give it a quick press with a steam iron before transferring the design, or spray it with clean water from your spray bottle and lightly press it with a warm iron. When you're finished with your embroidery, you may choose to press it again. Always keep your iron set very low so that you don't toast your embroidery or the linen twill. To protect your crewelwork while pressing, turn the crewelwork face down on a white terrycloth towel and cover it with a lightweight cotton cloth (such as a colorfast bandana, a kitchen towel, a handkerchief, or a press cloth). This helps to keep the design from getting flattened while pressing.

MEASURING TAPE, RULERS, AND CUTTING MATS

Every good embroiderer needs a classic dressmaker's measuring tape for measuring fabrics and thread. A T-square ruler is also helpful for making sure fabric cuts are always square. A plastic cutting mat with a measured grid drawn on one side, such as those used by quilters, is a perfect work surface for laying out small pieces of fabric. The mat will also withstand the impact of a pair of scissors, utility knife, or rotary blade.

STRAIGHT PINS

You should have some basic straight pins on hand to complete the projects in this book that require additional stitching. You'll need them for pinning various pieces and parts together.

NEW CREWEL TECHNIQUES

The following are some basic techniques you'll need to know in order to get started on your first crewel project.

TRANSFERRING A DESIGN

The best way to transfer a design from paper to fabric is the sunny window trick. Here's how it works. If you're using a design from this book, place a piece of tracing paper over the design in the book and trace the design onto the tracing paper with a felt-tip pen. Then take the tracing paper and tape it to a sunny window, making sure it's flat and secure on all sides. Next, tape your piece of linen twill (or whatever fabric you've chosen) squarely over the tracing paper. Using a fabric pen or pencil, trace the design again onto the fabric. Use short, light strokes so that the fabric doesn't shift over the tracing paper.

If you're lucky enough to have a professional light box (like photographers use), or if you have the do-it-yourself smarts to make your own, all the better. Follow the same instructions as above but omit the sunny window part!

All of the designs in this book may be reduced, enlarged, or repeated. Use a photocopier to make your own custom sizes and combinations.

HOOPING YOUR FABRIC

It's important to keep your fabric taut while you work so that there's no puckering in your crewelwork; careful hooping does the trick. Hoops come in two parts: the inner hoop, which is a continuous piece of wood, and the outer hoop, which has a screw connector for tightening your fabric between the two pieces. Lay the inner hoop on a flat surface and center your fabric on top of it with your design facing up. Loosen the screw on the outer hoop so that it's loose enough to easily place over the fabric that's sitting on the inner hoop (figure 1). Press the outer hoop down around the inner hoop until the fabric is evenly caught between the two hoops. Adjust the fabric as necessary and tighten the screw on the outer hoop until the fabric is taut like a drum (figure 2). The fabric will naturally loosen as you work, so you'll want to stop stitching occasionally and retighten your fabric in the hoop.

Although it's nice to be able to fit your design in the center of a hoop and not have to shift and re-hoop as you work, this only works with small designs. If you get into bigger projects, you may need to move the hoop as you finish an area. It's okay to let your finished crewel areas get pinched in the hoop as you work on other areas. The wrinkles will disappear in the end when you block your finished crewelwork. However, if you find you must leave your work for an extended time (days or weeks), undo the hoop, and let the fabric relax until you have time to come back to it. You'll be glad you did.

THREADING THE NEEDLE

It's a crewel but necessary step: inserting thread into a needle's tiny eye. Don't let this part of the process be a deal breaker. If you're new to the world of stitchery, take some time to learn how to thread a needle. With patience and practice, you'll be able to accomplish this seemingly impossible task—I promise! Just follow the steps below. If you don't get it at first, try it again, and again. You aren't allowed to give up!

Take the thread in your dominant hand while holding the needle in your other hand. Make a 1-inch (2.5 cm) loop at one end of the thread. Lasso it around the needle and tug the thread away from the needle to make a crease (figure 3). Slide the needle out and pinch the creased thread between your thumb and forefinger at the fold. Guide the folded tip of the thread through the eye of the needle (figure 4). If you're getting cross-eyed and can't seem to do it, keep your cool and know that a great little tool called a needle threader is available at most fabric stores. Whatever you do, don't get frustrated. Stick with it, and you'll be crewelin' like a pro!

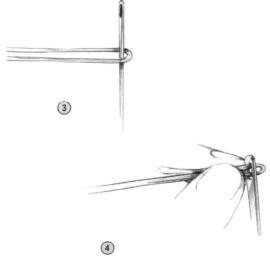

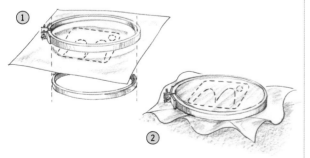

The CD included with this book conveniently gives you all the crewel motifs in digital form as color JPG files. Just pop the disc into your computer, and you'll be ready to go. You can easily resize and print out the motifs.

KNOTTING AND BEGINNING TO CREWEL

In crewelwork, it's traditional to have no knots in your finished work. But how do you start stitching if you can't tie a knot at the end of your thread? Here's how. After threading your needle, go ahead and make a knot at the end of the thread. Pick a spot on the front of your design that's about 2 inches (5 cm) from where you plan to begin stitching. At this spot, push your threaded needle through to the back. Yes, the knot will be on the front **(figure 5)**. Pull the thread taut and begin stitching your design. As you continue to sew, the thread that extends from the knot to where you started stitching will eventually get caught up and covered on the underside of the fabric. When this happens, it's safe to carefully trim off the knot from the front of your work **(figure 6)**. The rest of the thread will naturally slip to the back, and if there's still a bit dangling, you can trim it again.

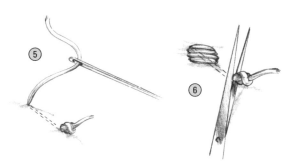

ENDING A THREAD

To end a thread, don't knot it. Remember: there are no knots in crewel (unless it's a French Knot). Instead, on the underside of your work, send the needle through several existing stitches without going through to the front **(figure 7)**. Do this back and forth two or three times. This will prevent the thread from pulling up on the front. After you've done this, trim any dangling threads. If you continue in this way, the underside of your crewelwork will stay smooth, have no tatters, and look almost as nice as the front.

Once you've used up a thread, begin a new one in the same way you just ended the last one. Pull the newly threaded needle through several existing stitches on the underside of your work. Repeat this until the thread feels secure. Continue stitching. Note that linen twill fabric is much sturdier than crewel wool thread, so if your thread wears thin or starts to break, end it right away and pick up where you left off with a fresh length of thread.

BLOCKING, PRESSING, AND FINISHING

There are a couple of ways to finish your crewelwork so that it's ready to be turned into something else—a pillow, framed art, or other project. The best way is to use the traditional blocking technique. Using this method, you stretch and square off your finished crewelwork on a wooden board, dampen it, and then let it dry. This works well and is very safe. The other way is slightly reckless, but it's quick and works for small pieces with designs that are no larger than 6 inches square (15 x 15 cm).

Here's the fast way: Lay your finished crewelwork face down on a terrycloth towel on top of an ironing board. Mist the crewelwork lightly with clean water from a spray bottle. Cover it with a thin piece of fabric, like a handkerchief. Using a medium warm iron, firmly press down on your embroidery, pulling the embroidered fabric at the corners as needed to make sure it stays in its original shape. You've got to work quickly so as not to scorch your work—just a couple of seconds of pressing at a time, enough to press out the wrinkles. Repeat until your crewelwork is dry.

Here's the recommended way: For traditional blocking, you'll need a clean board at least ¾ inch (2 cm) thick that's larger in height and width than your finished crewelwork, a piece of sturdy white cotton fabric about 8 inches (20.3 cm) bigger in width and length than your piece of wood, a box of 1-inch (2.5 cm) round-headed, rustproof nails, a staple gun, staples, and a hammer. Start by wrapping the wooden board with the cotton fabric and stapling all raw and folded edges to the underside of the board. Then lay your finished crewelwork face up on the board and center it. Starting in the center of the top edge of your crewelwork, tack a nail through the linen into the board. Only about ¼ inch (6 mm) of the nail needs to go into the board. Smoothing the fabric with your hands and stretching it as necessary, tack another nail through the center of the bottom edge. Do the same in the center of the left and right edges. Working from the centers to the corners, alternating top to bottom and then left to right, nail down the embroidery until all edges are secure. The spaces between each nail should be about 1 inch (2.5 cm). Be sure to keep the design square while you work. This may require stretching and pulling if your crewelwork lost its shape while you were embroidering. Next, spray your finished crewelwork with cold water until it's completely soaked. Set the board in a warm, airy place, and let the crewelwork dry. If you're in a hurry, use a fan or cool hairdryer to speed up the process. When your work is dry, remove the nails with a hammer or pliers. Your crewelwork should now be blocked and ready to frame or used in one of the projects featured in the last section of the book.

I've discovered another way to quickly and economically finish a piece of crewelwork. This method only works when the design is fully contained in a hoop, like all of the patterns in this book. Once you're finished stitching, re-center and re-tighten the crewelwork in the hoop. Tighten it some more, then spray it with clean water until the embroidery is soaked. Let the piece dry flat, face up. DO NOT remove it from the hoop. When the piece is dry, turn it over. While it's still in the hoop, trim the raw edge approximately 2 inches (5 cm) all the way around, leaving a 2-inch (5 cm) border. Then thread a sewing needle with 24 inches (60.9 cm) of a double thickness of hand-sewing thread. With the hoop's screw clasp at the top (12 o'clock) begin basting at 9 o'clock and continue clockwise, catching all of the fabric border until you get back to 9 o'clock. Gently pull the thread, gathering the fabric until it's fairly taut. Without letting the fabric get loose, insert the threaded needle at 3 o'clock and then at 9 o'clock again, going back and forth until the thread is too short and must be knotted **(figure 8)**. These long stitches across the back of the hooped crewelwork will allow you to hang the hoop on the wall like a picture. You can also unscrew the outer hoop and hang the finished piece as is. Either way, the piece makes a nice gift without the fuss of professional framing.

8

NEW CREWEL STITCHES

There are hundreds of crewel embroidery stitches. This section starts you out with just 19 of them, which are used in the projects in this book. Know that this is just a beginning. There are many more stitches to be learned, and many more still to be invented.

If you're familiar with embroidery but new to crewel, you'll be happy to know that the stitches are virtually the same. The main difference between crewel embroidery and other kinds of embroidery is the materials. Crewel is specifically done with two-ply worsted wool thread on linen fabric. Other types of embroidery use a myriad of materials from cottons to silks, including wool and linen.

If you've never embroidered before, I recommend practicing each stitch on a piece of scrap linen. When you're feeling confident, you can use the stitches as shown in the designs in the second part of the book. This section begins with the easy, breezy stitches, then progresses to the more advanced ones. I urge new crewelers to start at the beginning.

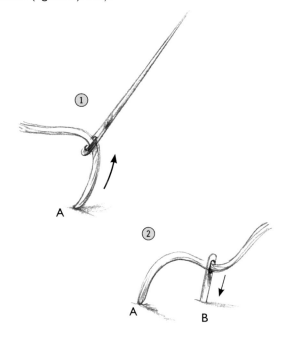

straight stitch

STRAIGHT STITCH

This is the simplest stitch in the whole crewel world. Send the threaded needle up from the back through to the front of your fabric at A **(figure 1)**. Then insert the needle down into the fabric front at B **(figure 2)**. Gently pull the threaded needle until the thread lies flat on the front of the fabric, and you're done **(figure 3)**. Easy.

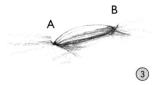

SEED STITCH

Seed stitch is made up of many very short Straight Stitches. Just as with Straight Stitch, send the threaded needle up from the back through the front of your fabric at A. Then insert the needle down into the fabric at B and pull through **(figure 4)**. Repeat **(figure 5)** again and again, making the stitches very close to each other but not touching, in random directions, until you've created a surface that looks like many little "seeds" **(figure 6)**.

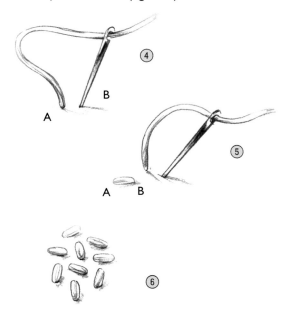

VARIATIONS

Make each Seed Stitch out of two or three stitches, one on top of the other, so that each Seed Stitch stands up off the fabric.

Seed Stitch is a good choice when you need the effect of shading in a design. Start on the edge that you want to be darker, making many Seed Stitches close together. Carefully thin them out until you have just a few on the side of your design that you want to look lighter. Voila!

BACK STITCH

Again, here's a stitch that's based on the Straight Stitch. Bring your threaded needle up at A and go down at B to make a straight stitch. Come up at C and go down at A again to make a second straight stitch **(figure 7)**. Come up again a stitch length ahead of C, then go down at C, and so on **(figure 8)** It's a bit like window shopping—two steps forward, one step back, two steps forward, one step back. As long as you keep going forward, you'll stay out of trouble. Note that Back Stitch can be done so that the stitches connect end-to-end as in **figure 8**, or with a small space between each stitch, as shown in the photograph at right.

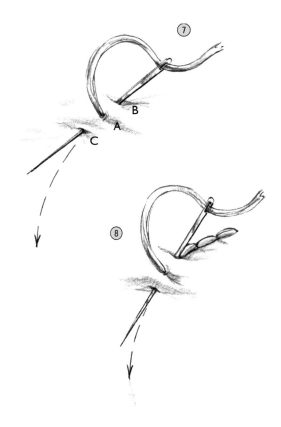

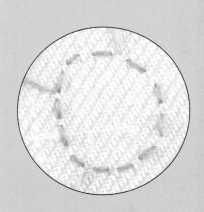

back stitch

SPLIT STITCH

This is a versatile "drawing" stitch, great for outlining designs. First, make a single Straight Stitch. Bring the needle up through the middle of your Straight Stitch at A, then go down at B **(figure 9)**. Come up at C, again "splitting" the stitch, and go down at D **(figure 10)**, and so on. Hint: Keep all of your stitches the same size except when stitching around a tight curve. Accommodate the curve by making your stitches much smaller. This will keep the flow of the line very smooth. Just like driving a car—it's smart to slow down when turning a corner.

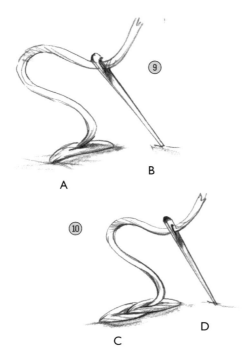

VARIATION

Stitch two lines of Split Stitch right next to each other to make an extra-thick line.

STEM STITCH/OUTLINE STITCH

Also known as Crewel Stitch or Stalk Stitch, this is one of the most basic and common of all crewel stitches. It works well for outlining, especially for lines that curve. And it moves fast! The final effect is a line of stitches that looks like a rope. There are two ways to do this stitch. In the first, the true Stem Stitch, you hold the thread with your thumb below the line of stitching. To begin, bring your threaded needle up at A. While going down at B and holding the thread down with your thumb on the outside of the curve, come up at C half way between A and B **(figure 11)**. Let go of the thread under your thumb and pull the thread taut, then go back down at D and up again at B, holding the thread down with your thumb **(figure 12)**. Repeat, keeping all of your stitches small and the exact same size **(figure 13)**. Outline Stitch, the second version of this stitch, is just like Stem Stitch, except that you hold the thread with your thumb above the line of stitching.

Keep the thread on the outside of the curve as you work, whether that's above or below the line of stitching. With either version, shorten your stitches when going around tight corners. This helps to make a cleaner, smoother line.

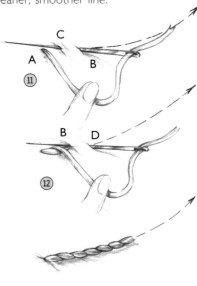

split stitch

CHAIN STITCH

Like Split Stitch, Stem Stitch, and Back Stitch, Chain Stitch works well as an outline stitch. Use it when you need a bolder line in your designs. First, bring your threaded needle up at A. Holding the thread down with your thumb, create a loop as you insert the needle very close to, but not into, A (**figure 14**). Bring the needle up through to the front of your fabric at B in the center of the loop (**figure 15**). Pull the thread to shorten the loop so it spans from A to B. Again, while holding the thread down with your thumb, create a loop as you insert the needle very close to, but not into, B (**figure 16**). Pull the thread again until the length of the second loop spans from B to C, and bring the needle up at C (**figure 17**). Insert the needle close to, but not into, C (**figure 18**). Repeat until you've created a "chain" out of these loops (**figure 19**). To end the chain, make a small stitch at the tip of the last loop.

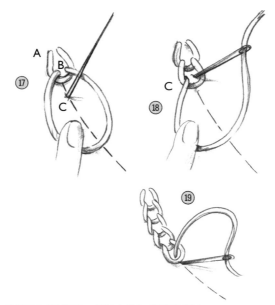

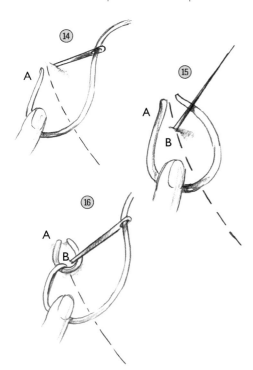

DETACHED CHAIN STITCH

Also known as the Daisy Stitch, the Detached Chain Stitch makes a perfect flower petal. First, bring your threaded needle up at A. Holding the thread down with your thumb, create a loop as you insert the needle back into A and in the same motion bring the needle up through to the front of your fabric at B inside of the loop (**figure 20**). Gently pull the thread to shorten the loop so it spans from A to B. (Don't pull too much or it won't look like a loop anymore.) Make a small stitch at the tip of the loop, or "petal" (**figures 21 and 22**).

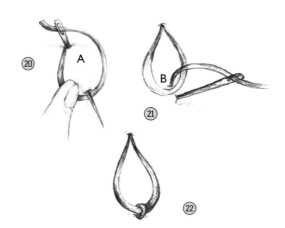

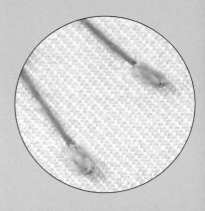

detached chain stitch

chain stitch

BLANKET STITCH

In crewelwork, Blanket Stitch is a simple but decorative linear stitch with unlimited variations. Begin by bringing your threaded needle up at A. Now, holding the thread down with your left thumb, send the needle down at B and come up at C. Keeping the yarn under the needle, pull the thread taut, forming a right angle **(figure 23)**. Send the needle down at D while holding the thread down with your left thumb coming up at E **(figure 24)**. Gently pull taut, forming another right angle, and repeat. **HINT:** For the best effect, try to keep the stitches the same length and the same distance apart, while maintaining an even tension.

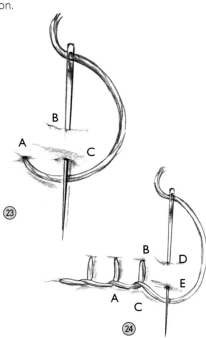

VARIATION

Make the length of the stitch from B to C longer than the stitch from D to E, and repeat over and over again to form a pattern.

SATIN STITCH

This is a classic embroidery stitch that looks easy but requires practice to master. The version of Satin Stitch that I use is one I discovered in a book by Erica Wilson. It's a combination of the Straight Stitch and the Split Stitch. First, use Split Stitch to outline the area to be filled with Satin Stitch **(figure 25)**. Then, beginning at the widest part of the shape you're filling, make Straight Stitches, one after the other, very close together, coming up at A, going down at B, coming up at C, going down at D, and so on **(figure 26)**. Hint: In order to get a soft, satiny finish, it's important to keep the tension of your thread the same throughout, not pulling too much or too little with each stitch **(figure 27)**.

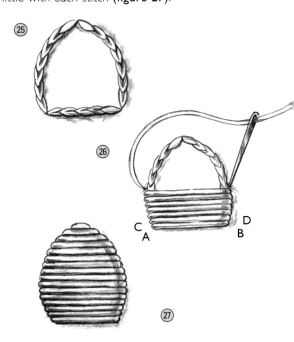

VARIATION

Make the Straight Stitches inside the Split Stitch outline as seen in Fiona's Flower on page 46.

satin stitch

SEPARATED SATIN STITCH

This stitch, which is related to regular Satin Stitch, is great for quickly getting color down with a loose, drawing-like quality. It's used in the Sea Anemone design on page 55. It's simple: Skip the underlying Split Stitch step and do Straight Stitches, one after the other, leaving a space between each stitch (figures 28 through 30).

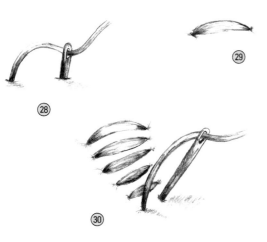

SATIN SHADING STITCH

Also known as the Long and Short Stitch or Soft Shading, this is the stitch that gives crewelwork its reputation of "painting with a needle and thread." Like Satin Stitch, this can be a tricky stitch to master, but it gives tremendous dimension to your designs when you get it right. It's similar to Satin Stitch in its application but requires at least three close shades of the same color thread to achieve the illusion of a shadow.

Begin by outlining the design area with Split Stitch. Starting at the lighter side of the design, using the lightest shade of thread, make a row of Satin Stitches in alternating lengths covering about one third of the outlined area (figure 31). Using the middle shade of

thread, make another row of alternating-length Satin Stitches, this time bringing the needle up through the ends of the first row of Satin Stitches (figure 32), covering the next third of the outlined area. Using the darkest shade of thread, make a final row of alternating-length Satin Stitches, again bringing the needle up through the ends of the second row of Satin Stitches, covering the rest of the outlined area (figure 33). HINT: When doing Satin Shading, always bring the needle UP through the last row of alternating-length Satin Stitches, not down. Also, Satin Shading works best when you use long stitches, close together and sometimes overlapping. As you work, keep an eye on the way the colors blend. Add random stitches as necessary in order to create the illusion of shading.

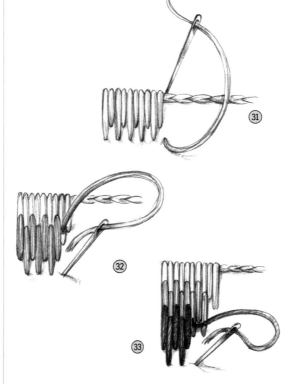

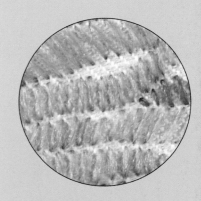

separated satin stitch

OVERCAST STITCH

This is a cool stitch for making a puffy line. Traditionally, it's suggested that you first do a line of separated Straight Stitches for your foundation (also known as Running Stitch). Instead, I recommend using Split Stitch. So, first, make a line out of Split Stitches (figure 34). Then make tiny, tiny Satin Stitches, one right after the other, completely covering the line of Split Stitch (figure 35).

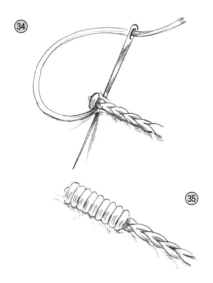

VARIATION

Make your foundation line extra thick with multiple lines of Split Stitch made right on top of each other. When you top that with Satin Stitch, you'll get a super-fat Overcast Stitch that will look really wormy on your fabric.

EYELET HOLE STITCH

I don't think this is specifically a crewel stitch, but I love it and find that it works well with crewel wool. Using Back Stitch, make a circle of stitching just inside the design line (figure 36). Using a knitting needle, a sewing stiletto, or the tip of a scissors, carefully punch a hole in the fabric inside your stitches (figure 37). If necessary, snip the fabric and trim close to the Back Stitch outline (figure 38). Next, using Overcast Stitch, send your threaded needle down through the hole in the center and come up at the edge of your design line, then down into the center and up again to form a stitch right next to the last one, covering the Back Stitch completely (figure 39). Continue in this way, making sure to keep your stitches very close together until you have gone all the way around the hole (figure 40).

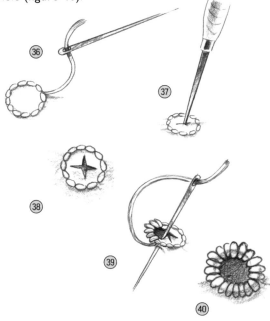

VARIATION

Make the width of the Overcast Stitch as thick or as thin as you like, or make it vary from thick to thin, creating a beautiful organic shape.

overcast stitch

SPIDERWEB STITCH

Also known as Circular Spider's Web or Whipped Spider's Web. It looks tricky, but it's really not. Go ahead—give it a spin! Starting from the outer edge of your design and working toward the center, use Straight Stitch to make "spokes" that will form the structure of the web (**figure 41**). Then slide the needle under spokes A and B near the center of the web (**figure 42**). Pull your thread taut. Again, slide the needle under spokes B and C. Pull your thread taut and toward the center of the web. Continue by sliding the needle under C and D and then under D and E (**figure 43**), and so on, filling the web from the center out (**figure 44**). Your web is finished when the spokes are no longer visible (**figure 45**).

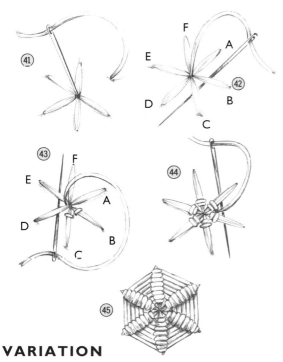

VARIATION

Stop weaving the web halfway up the spokes so that the spokes are partially exposed. And if you use a different color for the spokes, you'll get a really nice contrast.

CIRCULAR COUCHING STITCH

You can see this stitch in Spiny Spores on page 45 and Ella's Wish on page 59. First, make a series of Straight Stitches that share the edge of an arch or circle (**figure 46**). Then lace your thread underneath the Straight Stitches and pull it close to the arch, finishing at A (**figure 48**).

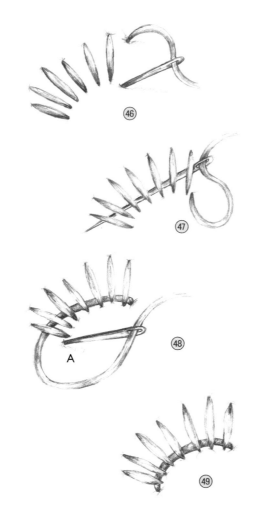

VARIATION

Use a bright, contrasting color for the underlying "couched" thread to create a subtle color play in your design.

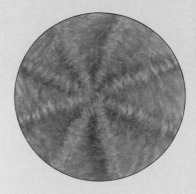

spiderweb stitch

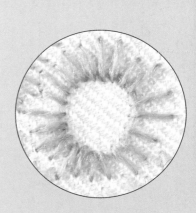

circular couching stitch

french knot

turkey work stitch

FRENCH KNOT

The French Knot is cool because it can be used as a single dot or done in multiples to fill an area. Bring your thread up to the front of your fabric at A. With the tip of the needle nearly touching the fabric at A, wrap the thread around the needle twice (**figure 50**). Insert the needle very near where it came up at A (**figure 51**). While pulling the thread nearly taut with your left hand, SLOWLY push the needle down through the fabric and pull taut on the underside. A knot will form on the surface (**figure 52**).

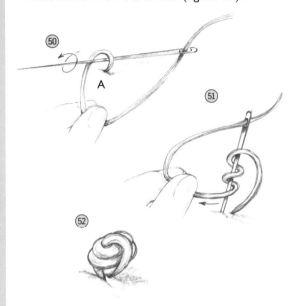

VARIATION

To make a smaller French Knot, wrap the thread around the needle only once. Similarly, wrap the thread three or four times to make it bigger.

TURKEY WORK

This is one of my new favorites. You can do it as a single fuzzy line of stitching like in the circles in Crewel Celia on page 36, or you can work in horizontal rows to fill a shape, creating the look of a tufted wool rug like I did in Zinnea on page 37. In fact, the stitch was originally used by rug makers in Turkey—thus the name Turkey Work. To begin, push your threaded needle in from the front at A. Without pulling the thread all the way through, leave a 1-inch (2.5 cm) "tail." Next, bring your needle up at B and go down at C. (**figure 53**). Then come up at A and, while holding the loop of thread down with your opposite hand's thumb, insert your needle at D (**figure 54**). Don't pull the thread taut. Next, come up at E and go down at B, this time pulling the thread taut (**figure 55**). Repeat this pattern—one loose stitch going forward and one tight stitch going backwards—over and over again until you reach the end of the shape you're filling (**figure 56**). Make another row of Turkey Work stitches very close and parallel to the first row. Continue in this way until you've filled the shape row after row. As you work, you can push down the rows of loops with your thumb to keep them out of your way. After you're done stitching, use a pair of scissors to evenly trim the loops, making a soft, velvety pile (**figure 57**). Use your needle or a fine comb to brush out the threads. **HINT:** The smaller and closer you make your stitches, the plusher it will be.

SQUARE FILLING STITCH

This stitch is perfect for adding texture and pattern to your crewel designs. Make several Straight Stitches running from opposite edges to form evenly spaced parallel lines **(figure 58)**. Repeat from the other two edges, creating a square grid **(figure 59)**. Using the same color or a contrasting color, make very small Straight Stitches at the intersections in the square grid until each intersecting pair of threads is tacked down **(figure 60)**.

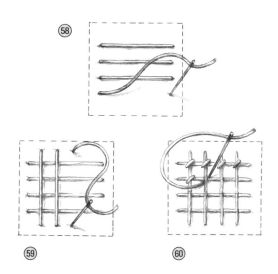

VARIATION

Add a French Knot in the center of each square in the grid.

CIRCULAR FILLING STITCH

This stitch is similar to the Square Filling Stitch and equally nice for quickly "filling" in large spaces with eye-catching patterns. First, you'll need to draw a circle of dots on your fabric. Then make long Straight Stitches that run from one side of the circle to the other starting at the top of the circle at A and going down at B **(figure 61)**. Work counter-clockwise until you've reached the top again. Up at C, down at D, up at E, and down at F, up at G, and down at H, and so on **(figure 62)**. Always leave the same number of dots between the beginning and end of each Straight Stitch. (In the illustration, I've skipped six dots for each Straight Stitch.) Using the same color or a contrasting color, make very small Straight Stitches at the intersections in the circular grid until each intersecting pair of threads is tacked down **(figure 63)**. Depending on how many dots you start with and how many dots you skip as you go around the circle, you'll have a wide-open circle center or a tightly closed circle center. There is no right or wrong. You can do this stitch in an infinite number of ways.

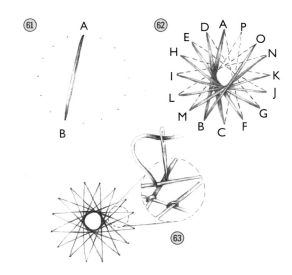

VARIATION

Use French Knots instead of tiny Straight Stitches to tack down the intersections.

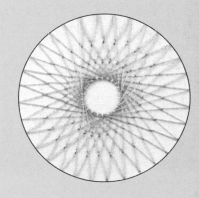

circular filling stitch

NEW CREWEL
GALLERY

Designs for my crewel patterns usually come straight from my own sketchbooks, which I carry with me wherever I go. For this collection, however, I took my inspiration from the colorful and whimsical drawings covering my refrigerator. I have two wee assistants, my daughter, Fiona Mae, and my son, Wyatt, who—like their mother—can't help but "color" from morning till night. Their drawings have truly been a source of inspiration for me, in both content and form. Over time, Wyatt's favorite color has morphed from straight-up orange to "rainbow," which is where it stands now. Consequently, you'll see lots of tangerine-colored crewel in this collection, as well as a rainbow piece.

Speaking of childhood, many of these designs were loosely inspired by the Spirograph, a very cool 1970s toy I had as a girl. To make these particular motifs, I took a simple circle of dots and connected them diagonally in a myriad of ways. Once

I started with the circle format, I was hooked. The results were magical, and the possibilities seemed endless. As a result, this collection is full of circular patterns—would-be flowers and other organic shapes found in nature. I hope you enjoy these new crewel designs and are inspired to create your own.

All of the designs in this chapter were embroidered using Appleton crewel wool thread with a size 24 chenille needle on Oyster White linen twill by the Ulster Linen Co. Pattern and stitch diagrams for these designs can be found starting on page 88. Each embroidery stitch is fully illustrated in the section on stitches, which begins on page 18. For instructions on enlarging and transferring the designs to fabric, and other notes on getting started, see the techniques section on page 14. For ideas on what to do with your finished crewelwork, check out the projects chapter on page 60.

Fabric
White linen twill, 9 inches square (22.75 x 22.75 cm)

Thread
Crewel wool, I skein each of pale kingfisher blue, medium sky blue, and split pea yellow*

Stitch
Split Stitch, Circular Filling Stitch, Straight Stitch

Finishing
Go to page 76 to see this design displayed with the others like delicate china plates on a wall.

Crewel Notes
This design offers endless possibilities. Explore different variations by simply increasing or decreasing the number of points on the circle's edge.

*I used Appleton crewel wool in colors 481, 562, and 997.

china blue - I

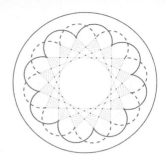

china blue - 2

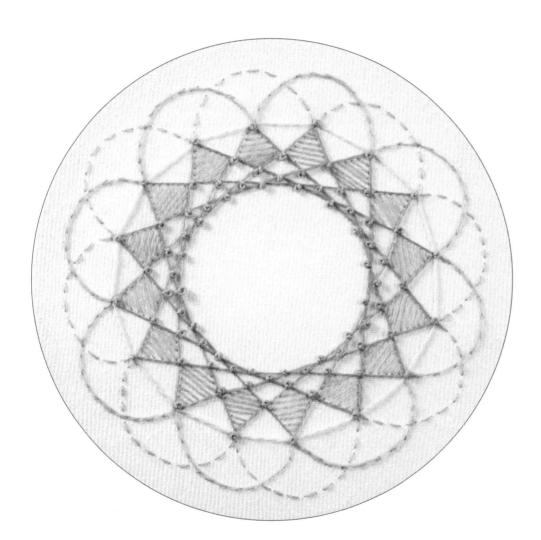

Fabric
White linen twill, 9 inches square (22.75 x 22.75 cm)

Thread
Crewel wool, 1 skein each of pale kingfisher blue, kingfisher blue, perfect sky blue, and split pea yellow*

Stitch
Split Stitch, Back Stitch, French Knot, Straight Stitch, Circular Filling Stitch

Finishing
Go to page 76 to see this design displayed with the others like delicate china plates on a wall.

Crewel Notes
To change the size of the circle formed in the middle, increase or decrease the number of points that you skip between the beginning and end of each long Straight Stitch on the circle's edge. The possibilities are limitless!

*I used Appleton crewel wool in colors 481, 483, 563, and 997.

Fabric

White linen twill, 9 inches square (22.75 x 22.75 cm)

Thread

Crewel wool, 1 skein each of periwinkle blue, pale kingfisher blue, light kingfisher blue, and split pea yellow*

Stitch

Split Stitch, French Knot, Circular Filling Stitch

Finishing

Go to page 76 to see this design displayed with the others like delicate china plates on a wall.

Crewel Notes

French Knots look a bit like tiny glass beads. Try using real beads to give your crewelwork a little sparkle.

*I used Appleton crewel wool in colors 462, 481, 482, and 997.

china blue - 3

china blue - 4

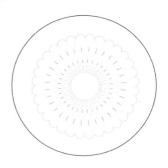

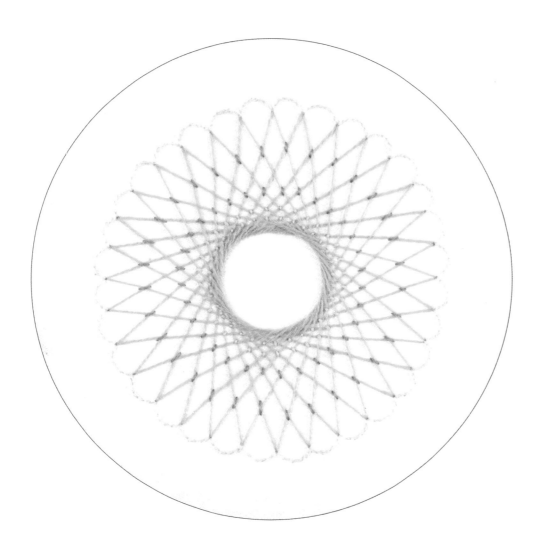

Fabric
White linen twill, 9 inches square (22.75 x 22.75 cm)

Thread
Crewel wool, 1 skein each of pale kingfisher blue, kingfisher blue, and split pea yellow*

Stitch
Split Stitch, Circular Filling Stitch

Finishing
Go to page 76 to see how you can display this design on a wall.

Crewel Notes
The tiny yellow stitches on top of the long blue stitches create a greenish glow. It's a subtle optical illusion. Squint, and maybe you'll see it!

*I used Appleton crewel wool in colors 481, 483, and 997.

Fabric
White linen twill, 9 inches square (22.75 x 22.75 cm)

Thread
Crewel wool, I skein each of pale kingfisher blue, kingfisher blue, medium kingfisher blue, deep king- fisher blue, medium sky blue, and split pea yellow*

Stitch
Circular Filling Stitch, Split Stitch, French Knot

Finishing
Go to page 76 to see this design displayed with the others like delicate china plates on a wall.

Crewel Notes
Changing the thread color from light to dark for the tiny stitches in this design will create a sense of depth.

*I used Appleton crewel wool in colors 481, 483, 484, 485, 562, and 997.

china blue - 5

china blue - 6

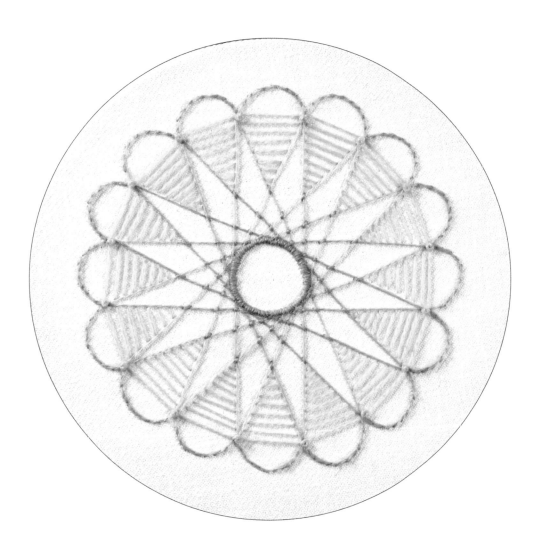

Fabric
White linen twill, 9 inches square (22.75 x 22.75 cm)

Thread
Crewel wool, I skein each of pale kingfisher blue, medium sky blue, and split pea yellow*

Stitch
Circular Filling Stitch, Split Stitch, French Knot, Straight Stitch, Overcast Stitch

Finishing
Go to page 76 to see this design displayed with the others like delicate china plates on a wall.

Crewel Notes
For an interesting and more complex pattern, pick three of the China Blue designs, enlarge one and shrink another, then repeat and slightly overlap them randomly on a large piece of linen.

*I used Appleton crewel wool in colors 481, 562, and 997.

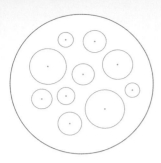

Fabric
White linen twill, 9 inches square (22.75 x 22.75 cm)

Thread
Crewel wool, 1 skein each of orange/red and light kingfisher blue*

Stitch
Turkey Work, French Knot

Finishing
Go to page 69 to see a pillow project inspired by this fuzzy design.

Crewel Notes
The pillows on page 69 don't include French Knots. Add them if you like!

*I used Appleton crewel wool in colors 444 and 482.

crewel cilia

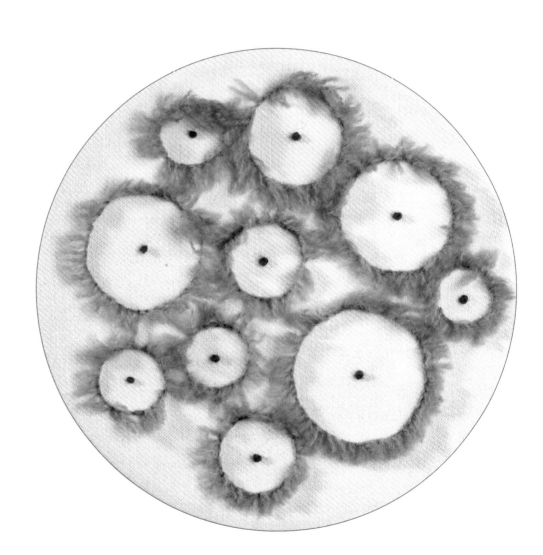

zinnea

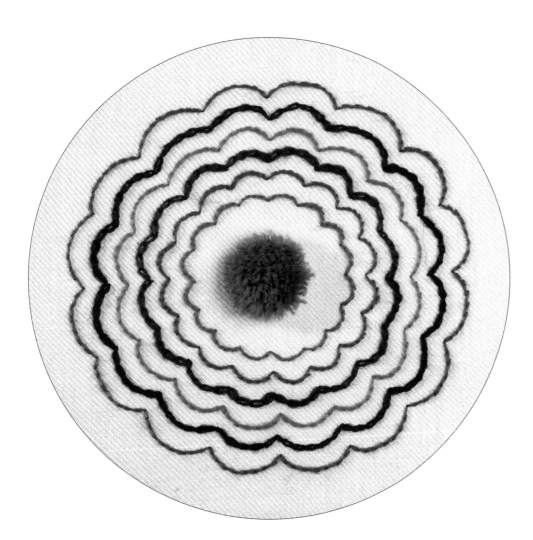

Fabric
White linen twill, 9 inches square (22.75 x 22.75 cm)

Thread
Crewel wool, I skein each of light orange, bright orange, bright orange/red, medium orange/red, deep orange/red, and kingfisher blue*

Stitch
Split Stitch, Chain Stitch, Turkey Work

Finishing
Go to page 82 to see how you can use this design to make a fancy pillow cover.

Crewel Notes
Doesn't the Turkey Work in this pattern look and feel like a wool rug? The stitch is often used to create an effect similar to that of a Turkish carpet. Hence the name Turkey Work.

*I used Appleton crewel wool in colors 441, 442, 443, 445, 446, and 483.

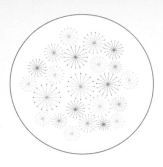

Fabric
White linen twill, 9 inches square (22.75 x 22.75 cm)

Thread
Crewel wool, 1 skein each of bright orange/red, pale orange, and orange*

Stitch
Straight Stitch

Finishing
How about stitching this design on the lower edge of a curtain?

Crewel Notes
For each Star, try to get all 16 Straight Stitches through the same center hole in the fabric, each time pushing the needle through the hole from the front of your crewelwork.

*I used Appleton crewel wool in colors 443, 622, and 862.

twinkling stars

firecracker

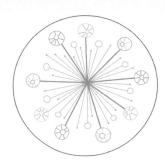

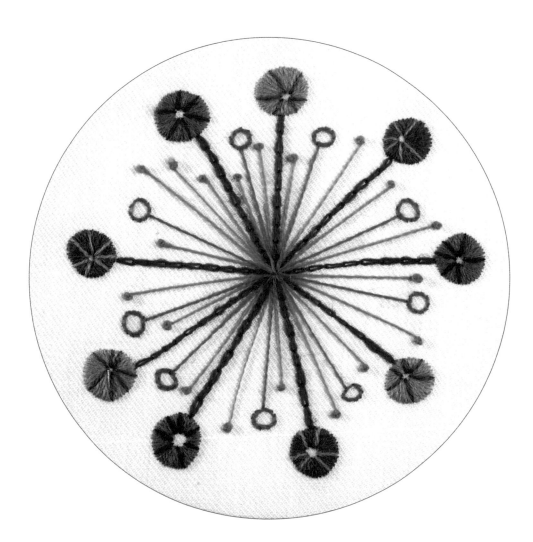

Fabric
White linen twill, 9 inches square (22.75 x 22.75 cm)

Thread
Crewel wool, I skein each of light orange, bright orange/red, medium orange/red, medium pink, pink, dark pink, and deep pink*

Stitch
Satin Stitch, Straight Stitch, Chain Stitch, Split Stitch, French Knot

Finishing
Go to page 65 to see how you can embroider this design on a pillow.

Crewel Notes
Begin by embroidering the Chain Stitch "spokes," then move on to the Split Stitch spokes, and so on.

*I used Appleton crewel wool in colors 441, 443, 445, 943, 944, 945, and 946.

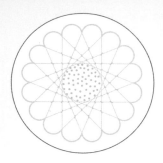

Fabric

White linen twill, 9 inches square (22.75 x 22.75 cm)

Thread

Crewel wool, I skein each of light yellow/orange, yellow/orange, and split pea yellow*

Stitch

Circular Filling Stitch, Split Stitch, French Knot

FInishing

Go to page 74 to see this design reworked on a blue, felted zipper purse.

Crewel Notes

For this design, do the Circular Filling Stitch first, then make a ring of French Knots around the outer edge of the flower's center, and work your way towards the middle.

*I used Appleton crewel wool in colors 554, 555, and 997.

sunflower

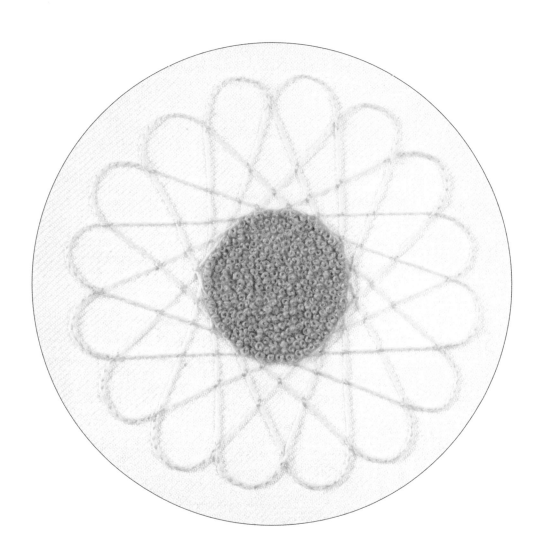

marigold

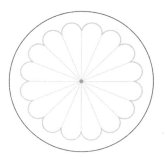

Fabric
White linen twill, 9 inches square (22.75 x 22.75 cm)

Thread
Crewel wool, I skein each of bright yellow and deep yellow/orange*

Stitch
Split Stitch, Straight Stitch, French Knot

Finishing
Try applying this design to a sewing basket top using the instructions on page 79. To see the design in white on a turquoise wraparound linen skirt, check out page 62.

Crewel Notes
Repeat this flower anywhere, but try not to make the long Straight Stitches any longer than two inches, as they can be easily snagged. If you're embroidering this design on something that will get a lot of use, add tiny couching stitches at one or two places on the long stitches. This will help to keep the long stitches down.

*I used Appleton crewel wool in colors 553 and 557.

Fabric
White linen twill, 9 inches square (22.75 x 22.75 cm)

Thread
Crewel wool, I skein each of light orange and bright yellow*

Stitch
Split Stitch, Straight Stitch, French Knot

FInishing
Go to page 79 to see how you can apply this design to a sewing basket top.

Crewel Notes
When making the long Straight Stitches in this design, work from the outside edge toward the center and try to get all of the stitches through the same center hole in the fabric. The French Knot comes last and goes through the same center hole.

*I used Appleton crewel wool in colors 441 and 553.

simple daisy

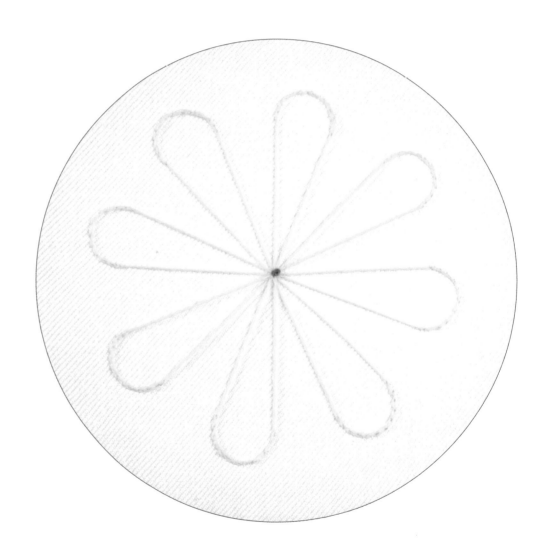

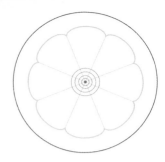

poppy

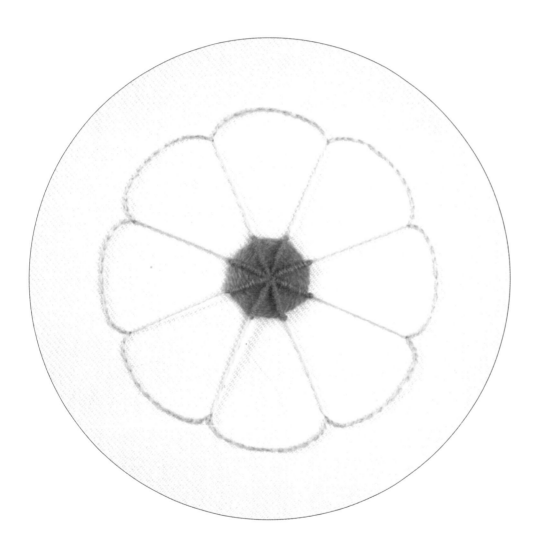

Fabric
White linen twill, 9 inches square (22.75 x 22.75 cm)

Thread
Crewel wool, I skein each of light kingfisher blue, yellow/orange, and deep yellow/orange*

Stitch
Split Stitch, Straight Stitch, Spiderweb Stitch, French Knot

Finishing
Go to page 79 to see how you can apply this design to a sewing basket top.

Crewel Notes
Do the long Straight Stitches first. Then, when you do the Split Stitch outline, come through the very tip of the long Straight Stitches, "splitting" each one to make it look as if it's part of the Split Stitch outline.

*I used Appleton crewel wool in colors 482, 555, and 557.

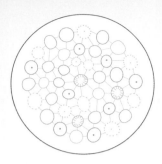

Fabric

White linen twill, 9 inches square (22.75 x 22.75 cm)

Thread

Crewel wool, 1 skein each of light spring green, pale green, light green, pale mint green, light sage green, sage green, and split pea yellow*

Stitch

Split Stitch, Back Stitch, Satin Stitch, Straight Stitch, French Knot

Finishing

Try framing this design in a shadow box like a scientific specimen.

Crewel Notes

This design was inspired by a board game my 4-year-old son made up. It reminds me of Chinese checkers, a game that I played as a child.

*I used Appleton crewel wool in colors 251A, 421, 422, 431, 482, 542, 543, and 997.

seed samples

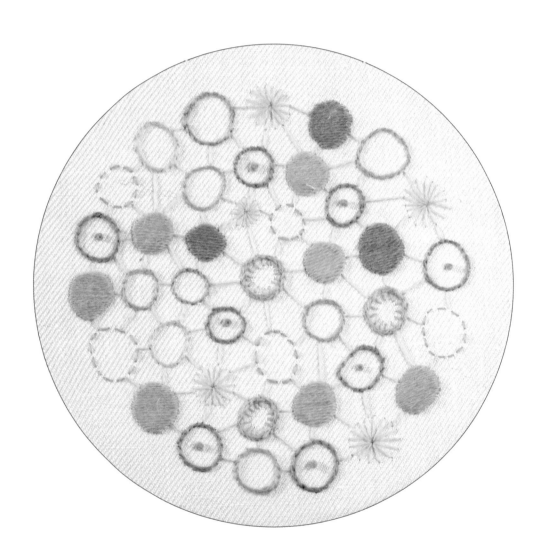

spiny spores

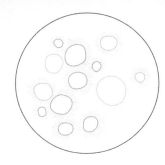

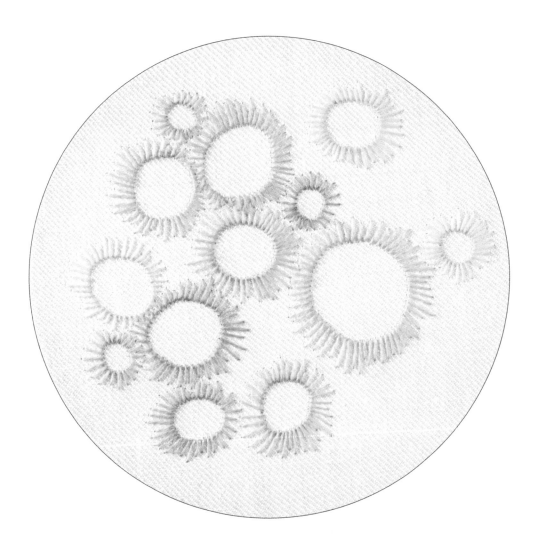

Fabric
White linen twill, 9 inches square (22.75 x 22.75 cm)

Thread
Crewel wool, 1 skein each of light spring green, light yellow/green, light green, pale mint green, pale sage green, light sage green, and pastel green*

Stitch
Circular Couching

Finishing
Go to page 62 to find out how you can add Spiny Spores to the edge of a linen skirt.

Crewel Notes
The Circular Couching stitch can be done in just about any shape. Instead of circles, try triangles, squares, hexagons, or octagons.

*I used Appleton crewel wool in colors 251A, 331, 422, 431, 541, 542, and 874.

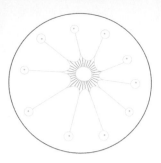

Fabric
White linen twill, 9 inches square (22.75 x 22.75 cm)

Thread
Crewel wool, 1 skein each of light spring green, pale kingfisher blue, light kingfisher blue, and split pea yellow*

Stitch
Split Stitch, Satin Stitch, French Knot

Finishing
Creative ideas for using your finished embroidery appear in the projects section, which starts on page 60.

Crewel Notes
For this design, do the yellow Split Stitch first, then do the Satin Stitch inside the Split Stitch outline without stitching over the Split Stitch outline. See page 22 for details on this variation.

*I used Appleton crewel wool in colors 251A, 481, 483, and 997.

fiona's flower

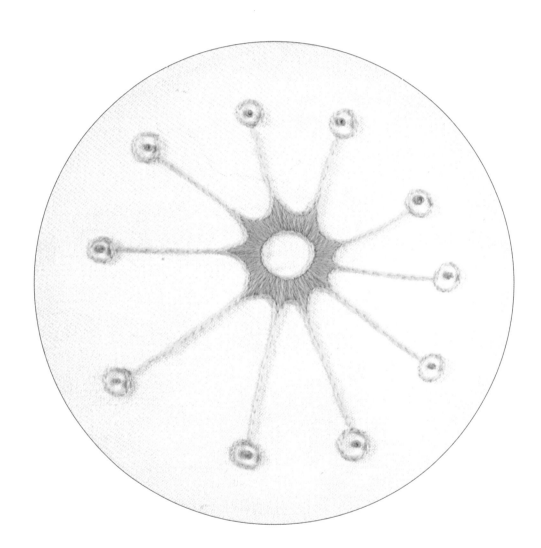

lazy daisy

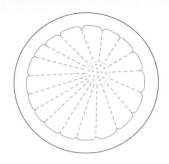

Fabric
White linen twill, 9 inches square (22.75 x 22.75 cm)

Thread
Crewel wool, I skein each of pale kingfisher blue, light kingfisher blue, pale yellow, yellow, and split pea yellow*

Stitch
Split Stitch, Back Stitch, French Knot

Finishing
Creative ideas for using your finished embroidery appear in the projects section, which starts on page 60.

Crewel Notes
For this design, make the petals first, then do a ring of French Knots around the outer edge of the flower's center and work your way toward the middle, changing the thread color as indicated on the diagram.

*I used Appleton crewel wool in colors 481, 482, 551, 552, and 997.

Fabric
White linen twill, 9 inches square (22.75 x 22.75 cm)

Thread
Crewel wool, 1 skein each of gray and bright white*

Stitch
"Double" Split Stitch, Straight Stitch, French Knot

FInishing
Go to page 82 to see this design embroidered on a turquoise blue pillow cover.

Crewel Notes
"Double" Split Stitch is made from two lines of Split Stitch embroidered very close to each other. Try three or four lines, or use a different shade of one color for each line of Split Stitch to create an interesting, vibrating edge.

*I used Appleton crewel wool in colors 988 and 991B.

delicate doily

hollyhock

Fabric
White linen twill, 9 inches square (22.75 x 22.75 cm)

Thread
Crewel wool, 1 skein each of light orange, bright orange/red, medium orange red, and light kingfisher blue*

Stitch
Satin Stitch, Straight Stitch, French Knot

Finishing
Go to page 82 to see how you can use this design to make a pillow cover.

Crewel Notes
When doing Satin Stitch "in the round," as in this design, be sure to space the stitches closer together on the inside edges than on the outer edges. "Fanning" the stitches in this way will help keep them even and parallel as you work your way around the design. Take it easy. Practice makes perfect!

*I used Appleton crewel wool in colors 441, 443, 445, and 482.

mirabella

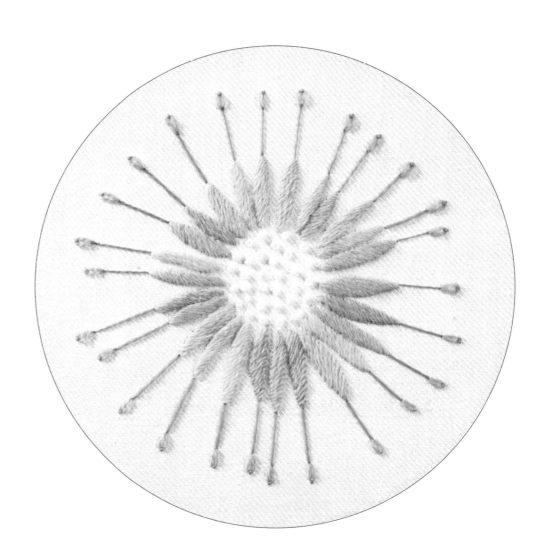

Fabric
White linen twill, 9 inches square (22.75 x 22.75 cm)

Thread
Crewel wool, 1 skein each of light spring green, light yellow/green, pale green, light green, pale sage green, deep yellow/orange, pale orange, and cream white*

Stitch
French Knot, Straight Stitch, Satin Stitch, Detached Chain Stitch

Finishing
This design is similar in color and style to Seed Samples (page 44), Spring Anemone (page 56), and Spiny Spores (page 45).

Crewel Notes
As I was finishing this pattern, my friend Mira came to watch. She was curious about my handiwork, but I was intrigued by her eyes, which are speckled with the same greens as the ones in this design. To Mira!

*I used Appleton crewel wool in colors 251A, 331, 421, 422, 541, 557, 622 and 992.

beaded bobbles

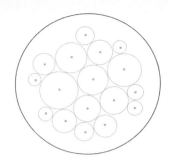

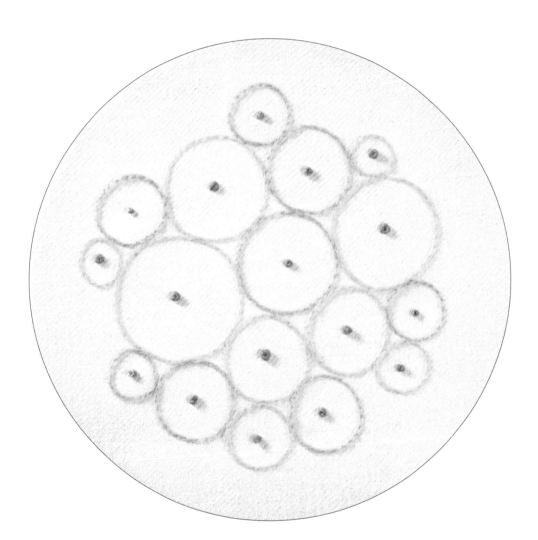

Fabric
White linen twill, 9 inches square (22.75 x 22.75 cm)

Thread
Crewel wool, I skein each of pale green, light green, pale orange, and orange*

Stitch
Satin Stitch, Split Stitch, French Knot

Finishing
This is another pattern that could go on and on. Imagine a bed quilt covered with these circles and knots. Don't stop!

Crewel Notes
Most of the patterns in this book are stitched on linen twill. This is my favorite surface to do crewel embroidery on because it's sturdy and smooth. But several light-weight linen plain weaves are available that are better for embroidered clothing projects like skirts, shirts, aprons, and dresses.

*I used Appleton crewel wool in colors 421, 422, 622, and 862.

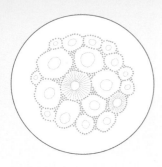

Fabric
White linen twill, 9 inches square (22.75 x 22.75 cm)

Thread
Crewel wool, 1 skein each of deep yellow/orange, pale orange, and orange*

Stitch
Straight Stitch, French Knot

Finishing
This design would be especially cool embroidered on a pillow.

Crewel Notes
The French Knot can be made by wrapping the thread once, twice, or three times to create small, medium, or large knots. I executed this design primarily with twice-wrapped knots, but because of the organic nature of the pattern, I also used ones and threes to help fill in the uneven spaces.

*I used Appleton crewel wool in colors 557, 622, and 862.

seed pod

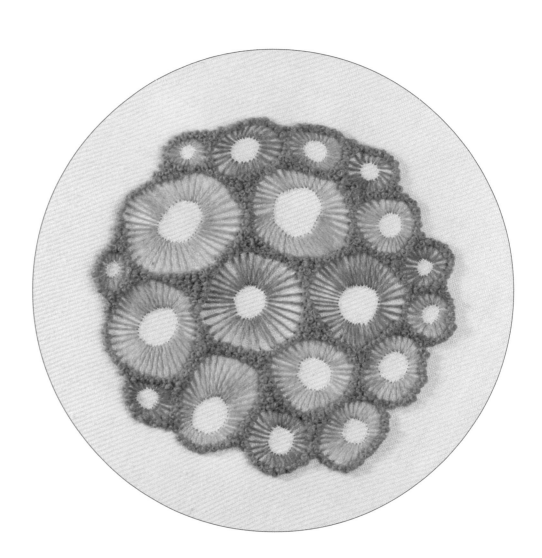

malia's maze

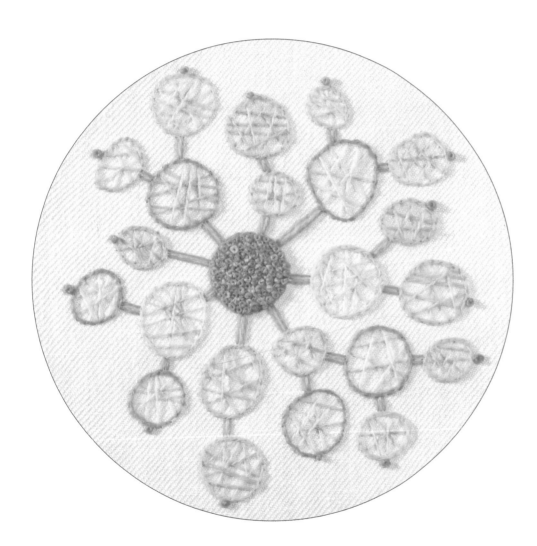

Fabric
White linen twill, 9 inches square (22.75 x 22.75 cm)

Thread
Crewel wool, 1 skein each of light spring green, light yellow/green, pale green, light green, bright yellow, light yellow/orange, yellow/orange, bright yellow/orange, deep yellow/orange, and pastel green*

Stitch
French Knot, Split Stitch, Straight Stitch

Finishing
This design could go on and on, like a wild weed in an abandoned garden. Start with a bigger piece of linen and keep attaching more orange and yellow circular shapes.

Crewel Notes
My niece, Malia, helped me come up with this pattern during a long ride to the beach. Crewel's great for passing the time in the car!

*I used Appleton crewel wool in colors 251A, 331, 421, 422, 553, 554, 555, 556, 557, and 874.

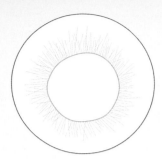

Fabric
White linen twill, 9 inches
square (22.75 x 22.75 cm)

Thread
Crewel wool, 1 skein each
of bright yellow/orange,
pale orange, and orange*

Stitch
Straight Stitch, Split Stitch

Finishing
Embroider this fun design
on a linen tea towel.
Change up the colors to
match your kitchen.

Crewel Notes
For this design, do the
Straight Stitches first, then
finish with the Split Stitch
circle.

*I used Appleton crewel
wool in colors 556, 622,
and 862.

cosmic burst

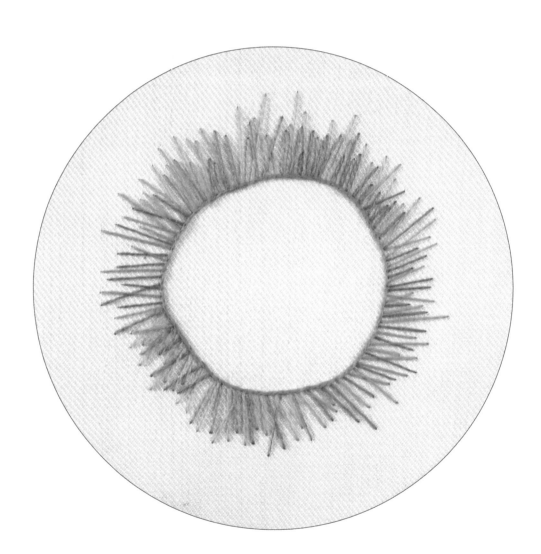

sea anemone

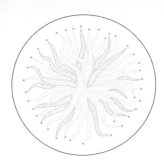

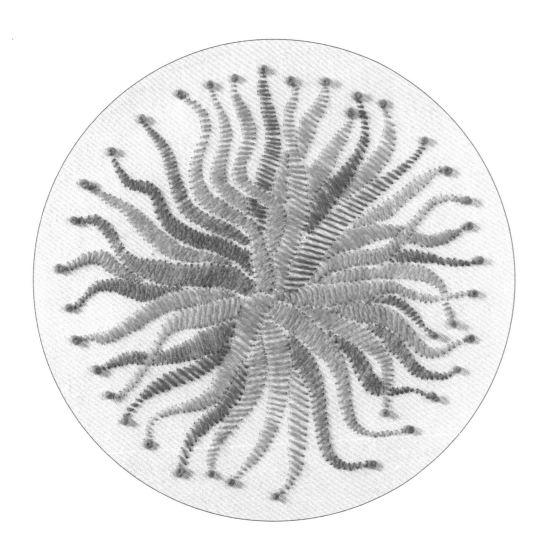

Fabric
White linen twill, 9 inches square (22.75 x 22.75 cm)

Thread
Crewel wool, 1 skein each of light orange, deep yellow/orange, pale orange, and orange*

Stitch
French Knot, Separated Satin Stitch

Finishing
This design was inspired by a fish-eating sea anemone called Tealia. How about stitching it on the front of a large canvas beach bag?

Crewel Notes
The Separated Satin Stitch, the main stitch used in this design, works well for creating a loose, drawn effect.

*I used Appleton crewel wool in colors 441, 557, 622, and 862.

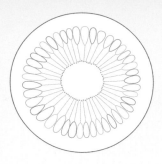

Fabric

White linen twill, 9 inches square (22.75 x 22.75 cm)

Thread

Crewel wool, 1 skein each of light spring green, pale green, light green, pale mint green, light orange, sage green, and deep yellow/orange*

Stitch

Split Stitch, Straight Stitch, French Knot

Finishing

Try enlarging this design and embroidering it on a throw pillow.

Crewel Notes

For more crewel facts, check out *The New Crewel* (Lark Crafts, 2005), the first book on contemporary crewel embroidery. It's chock-full of crewel ideas, tips, and patterns.

*I used Appleton crewel wool in colors 251A, 421, 422, 431, 441, 543, and 557.

spring anemone

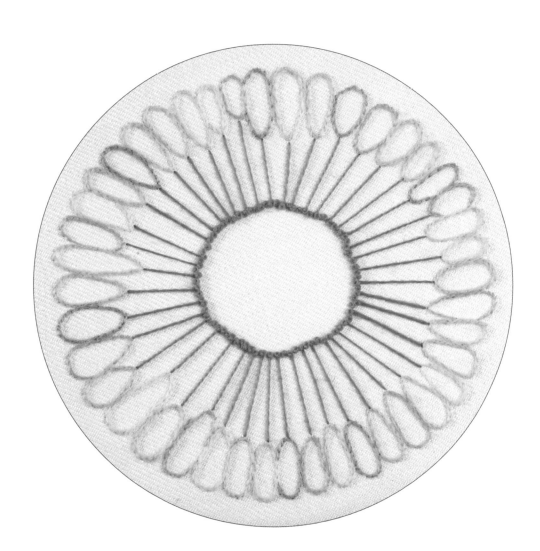

dahlia

Fabric
White linen twill, 9 inches square (22.75 x 22.75 cm)

Thread
Crewel wool, I skein each of yellow, light yellow/orange, yellow/orange, bright yellow/orange, deep yellow/orange, and split pea yellow*

Stitch
Split Stitch

Finishing
Wouldn't this design be nice done in shades of bright fuchsia and hot pink on a white linen table-cloth?

Crewel Notes
When using Split Stitch on tight curves like the ones in this design, make sure your stitches are extra tiny so the curved lines are smooth.

*I used Appleton crewel wool in colors 552, 554, 555, 556, 557, and 997.

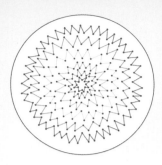

Fabric
White linen twill, 9 inches square (22.75 x 22.75 cm)

Thread
Crewel wool, I skein each of light green, light orange, deep orange/red, periwinkle blue, light kingfisher blue, and light yellow/orange*

Stitch
Straight Stitch

Finishing
Try this—or any other rainbow-inspired design—on blue jeans. No pattern required. Just do zigzags till you feel like you've had enough.

Crewel Notes
This one's for my 4-year-old son, Wyatt, who's obsessed with rainbows. May he never outgrow them.

*I used Appleton crewel wool in colors 422, 441, 446, 462, 482 and 554.

wyatt's rainbow

ella's wish

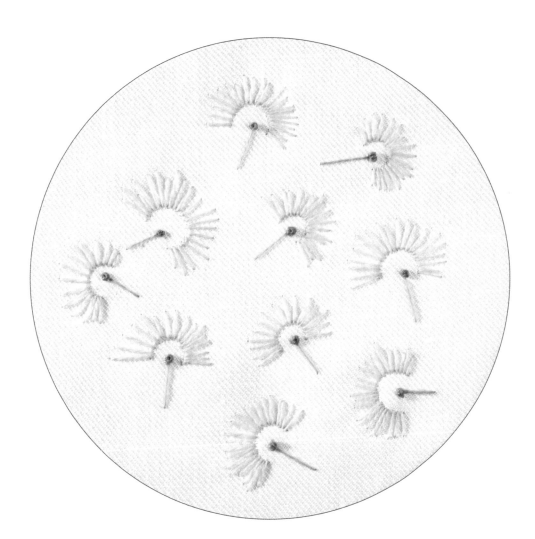

Fabric
White linen twill, 9 inches square (22.75 x 22.75 cm)

Thread
Crewel wool, I skein each of light spring green, light yellow/green, pale king-fisher blue, light kingfisher blue, and grey*

Stitch
French Knot, Straight Stitch, Circular Couching

Finishing
This pattern reminds me of making a wish while blowing out the seedlings of a dandelion. It's perfect for cloth picnic napkins.

Crewel Notes
When doing the Circular Couching Stitch in this design, stitch all of the light spring green straight stitches first, leaving a few random spaces in between. Then create the grey straight stitches. Finally, "thread" the light yellow/green wool taut underneath the straight stitches.

*I used Appleton crewel wool in colors 251A, 331, 481, 482, and 988.

New Crewel

NEW CREWEL
PROJECTS

When it comes to embellishment, the crewel motifs in this book have countless applications. You can use them to make stand-out accessories, delightful décor, and more. The easy-to-complete projects in this chapter will show you how. Don't be afraid to get creative! Let the projects in this section inspire you. Follow the directions as they're presented or use them as starting points. Change them up by substituting any of the crewel motifs featured in the book's gallery section. You can also choose different backgrounds to work on. While I prefer classic white linen twill for most of my crewelwork, I also like the look and feel of plain-weave linens in vibrant colors (see the Wraparound Linen Skirt on page 62 and the Blossom Sewing Basket on page 79). Light-colored wool threads really pop when stitched on darker fabrics. Try mixing textures and materials. I did one project on a felted wool purse and another on old aluminum screening. You can easily customize each project to make a finish product that's all your own. Think outside the hoop!

wraparound linen skirt

With a few simple stitches, you can transform a plain
linen skirt into a one-of-a-kind wearable.

Patterns

Marigold (see page 96)
Twinkling Stars (see page 98)

Stitches

Straight Stitch, Split Stitch,
French Knot

What You Need

Turquoise (or color of your choice) linen skirt

Hoop, 6 to 8 inches (15.2 to 20.3 cm) in diameter

*Crewel wool thread, 2 skeins of cream white or color of
your choice*

*Chenille needle, size 24, or comparable crewel needle
of choice*

1 quarter (25-cent piece)

Fabric pen (the vanishing kind)

Scissors

Instructions

1 Lay your skirt on a flat surface and smooth out
all the wrinkles.

2 Using the vanishing fabric pen, transfer the
Marigold and Twinkling Stars patterns randomly
and repeatedly across the lower edge of the linen
skirt front (see page 14). Draw a sprinkling of dots
throughout the design. The dots will be where you
stitch the French Knots.

3 Use the vanishing pen to trace the quarter,
drawing circles randomly throughout the design.
The complete design should cover approximately
8 to 12 inches (20.3 to 30.5 cm) of the lower front
edge of the skirt.

4 Hoop a portion of the skirt's edge (see page 15).

5 Knot and thread the needle and embroider the
stitches as indicated in the diagrams for Marigold
and Twinkling Stars.

6 Unscrew and rehoop your fabric as you finish
one area and move onto the next.

7 After stitching the entire front, block your finished crewelwork using a hot iron and water from a spray bottle (see page 16).

VARIATIONS

Use the other designs in this book to transform a tea towel, curtain, or pair of blue jeans.

I used Appleton crewel wool in color 992.

firecracker pillow cover

This easy-to-execute pattern really pops! Add some spark to your living space by stitching it on a pillow cover.

Pattern

Firecracker (see page 99)

Stitches

Split Stitch, Chain Stitch, Satin Stitch, Straight Stitch Overlay, French Knots

What You Need

Natural plain linen, 20 inches square (50.8 x 50.8 cm)

Coordinating cotton or linen fabric, 2 pieces, each 16 x 12 inches (40.5 x 30.5 cm)

White cotton fabric for lining, 1 piece 16 inches square (40.5 x 40.5 cm) and 2 pieces, each 16 x 12 inches (40.5 x 30.5 cm)

Hoop, 8 to 10 inches (20.3 to 25.4 cm) in diameter

Crewel wool thread, 1 skein each of light orange, bright orange/red, medium orange/red, medium pink, pink, dark pink, and deep pink

Chenille needle, size 24, or comparable crewel needle of choice

Pillow form, 14 inches square (35.5 x 35.5 cm)

Tracing paper

Fabric pen or pencil

Scissors

Straight pins

Ruler

Sewing thread

Hand-sewing needle

Instructions

1. Using the tracing paper and the fabric pen or pencil, transfer the Firecracker pattern onto the center of the piece of 20-inch-square (50.8 x 50.8 cm) natural linen fabric (see page 14).

2. Hoop the design (see page 15) and embroider it using the colors and stitches as indicated in the Firecracker diagram.

3. Block your finished crewelwork (see page 16).

4. Trim 2 inches (5 cm) from each side of your embroidery, leaving a 1-inch (2.5 cm) border on all sides. The linen fabric with finished crewelwork should now measure 16 x 16 inches (40.5 x 40.5 cm).

5. Lay your crewelwork face down on a flat surface. Lay the large piece of lining fabric on top of your crewelwork. Pin the two pieces of fabric together and baste with the sewing thread and hand sewing needle, using a series of long, 1- to 2-inch (2.5 to 5 cm) straight stitches in diagonal rows spaced about 3 inches (7.5 cm) apart (fig. 1). Don't make these stitches too tight, since you'll remove them later. Set aside.

6. Lay one of the 16 x 12 inch (40.5 x 30.5 cm) pillow back pieces of coordinating fabric on a flat surface. Place one of the 16 x 12 inch (40.5 x 30.5 cm) pieces of cotton lining fabric on top of the coordinating fabric. Pin together and baste as described above. Repeat for the second piece of pillow back and lining fabric.

7. For each pillow back piece, fold one long edge 1 inch (2.5 cm) in toward the lining. Press with a hot iron, or form a crease by rubbing your fingers along the fold. Fold again another 1 inch (2.5 cm), press or crease with your fingers, and pin along the folded edge (fig. 2).

8. Using the sewing thread, run a line of Blanket Stitch along the inside folded edge on each of the pieces (fig. 3). Remove the pins. You should now have two 16 x 10-inch (40.5 x 25.4 cm) pieces of basted, lined, and hemmed fabric that will be used to make the backing for your pillow.

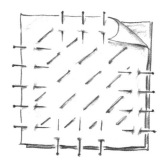

figure 1

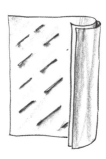

figure 2

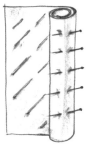

figure 3

9 Lay your basted and lined crewelwork face up on a flat surface. Lay one of the small pieces face down on top of the crewelwork with the fold in the middle and the left edges lining up *(fig. 4)*. Pin the left edges together. Lay the other small piece in the same manner matched to the right side edge of the crewelwork, and pin the right side edges. The two folded and hemmed edges now overlap in the center *(fig. 5)*.

10 Pin the top and bottom edges, and place a few pins through the center where the two smaller pieces overlap. Flip your work so that the lining side of the crewelwork is facing up.

11 Using the sewing thread and Back Stitch, stitch the three pieces together leaving a 1-inch (2.5 cm) hem on all sides. Remove all of the pins.

12 Trim the seam allowances to ½ inch (1.25 cm).

13 Trim the corners, being careful not to cut too close to the stitching *(fig. 6)*.

14 Remove the basting stitches.

15 Turn the pillow right side out.

16 Using the end of a blunt scissors, a knitting needle, or chopsticks, gently push out corners. Be careful not to push too hard, or you'll poke a hole in your work.

17 Slip in the pillow form and adjust.

VARIATIONS

Do the same design, but in different colors. How about all blues or whites?

I used Appleton crewel wool in colors Appleton 441, 443, 115, 943, 944, 945, and 946.

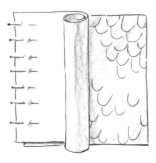

figure 4

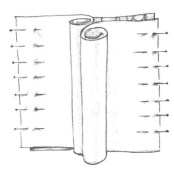

figure 5

figure 6

crewel cilia pillows

Featuring the Turkey Work stitch—so called
because it was originally used by rug makers in Turkey—
these appliquéd pillows will amp up the appeal of any room.

What You Need

White linen twill, 18 x 22 inches (45.7 x 55.8 cm)

*Orange linen plain weave, 2 pieces, each 14 x 12 inches
(35.5 x 30.4 cm)*

*White cotton fabric for lining, 1 piece 18 x 22 inches
(45.7 x 55.8 cm) and 2 pieces, each 14 x 12 inches
(35.5 x 30.4 cm)*

*12 coordinating cotton or linen fabric circles, each approx-
imately 1¾ inches (4.4 cm) in diameter*

Hoop, 6 to 10 inches (15.2 to 25.4 cm) in diameter

*Crewel wool thread, 1 skein each of light spring green
and light kingfisher blue*

*Chenille needle, size 24, or comparable crewel needle of
choice*

2 pillow forms, each 12 x 16 inches (30.4 x 40.6 cm)

Tracing paper

Fabric pen or pencil

Scissors

Straight pins

Ruler

Sewing thread

Hand-sewing needle

Instructions

1 Using the fabric pen or pencil, draw approximately six circles 1 to 3 inches (2.54 to 7.6 cm) in
diameter on the white linen fabric (see page 70 for
finished pillow).

2 Turn the edges of one of the coordinating fabric circles under approximately ¼ inch (0.6 cm) all
around. Press the folded edges with a hot iron or
crease them with your fingers. Repeat with five of
the fabric circles.

3 Pin each fabric circle, right side up, in the spaces around the circles drawn on the white linen.

4 Using either the light spring green thread or
another color of your choice to match your circle
fabric, stitch the circles into place with little Straight
Stitches. Press these appliquéd circles with a hot iron.

5 Starting with the top left section of the design,
hoop a portion of the fabric (see page 15). Work
on one Turkey Work circle at a time, unscrewing
the hoop and rehooping as you complete a circle.

6 Embroider the design, using colors and stitches
as indicated in the Crewel Cilia diagram.

7 Block your finished crewelwork (see page 16).

8 Trim 2 inches (5 cm) from each side of your embroidery, leaving a 1-inch (2.5 cm) border on all sides. The linen fabric with finished crewelwork should now measure 14 x 18 inches (35.5 x 45.7 cm).

9 Lay your crewelwork face down on a flat surface. Lay the large piece of lining fabric on top of your crewelwork. Pin the two pieces of fabric together and baste with the sewing thread and the hand sewing needle, using a series of long, 1 to 2 inch (2.5 to 5 cm) straight stitches in diagonal rows spaced about 3 inches (7.5 cm) apart. Don't make these stitches too tight since you'll remove them later. Set aside.

10 Lay one of the 14 x 12 inch (35.5 x 30.5 cm) pillow back pieces of orange linen fabric on a flat surface. Place one of the 14 x 12 inch (35.5 x 30.5 cm) pieces of lining fabric on top of the linen fabric. Pin together and baste as described above. Repeat for the second piece of pillow back and lining fabric.

11 For each pillow back piece, fold one long edge 1 inch (2.5 cm) in toward the lining. Press with a hot iron or form a crease by rubbing your fingers along the fold. Fold again another 1 inch (2.5 cm), press or crease with your fingers, and pin along the folded edge.

12 Using the sewing thread, run a line of Blanket Stitch along the inside folded edge on each of the pieces. Remove the pins. You should now have two 14 x 10-inch (35.5 x 25.4 cm) pieces of basted, lined, and hemmed fabric that will be used to make the backing for your pillow.

13 Lay your basted and lined crewelwork face up on a flat surface. Lay one of the small pieces face down on top of the crewelwork, with the fold in the middle and the left edges lining up. Pin the left edges together. Lay the other small piece in the same manner matched to the right side edge of the crewelwork, and pin the right side edges. The two folded and hemmed edges now overlap in the center.

14 Pin the top and bottom edges and place a few pins through the center where the two smaller pieces overlap. Flip your work so that the lining side of the crewelwork is facing up.

15 Using the sewing thread and Back Stitch, stitch the three pieces together leaving a 1-inch (2.5 cm) hem on all sides. Remove all of the pins.

16 Trim the seam allowance to ½ inch (1.25 cm).

17 Trim the corners, being careful not to cut too close to the stitching.

18 Remove the basting stitches.

19 Turn the pillow right side out.

20 Using the end of a blunt scissors, a knitting needle, or chopsticks, gently push out corners. Be careful not to push too hard or you'll poke a hole in your work.

21 Repeat steps 1-20 for the other pillow.

22 Slip in the pillow forms.

VARIATION

Comb out the threads left from the Turkey Work Stitch until they're frizzy.

I used Appleton crewel wool in colors 482 and 251A.

Pattern

None other than a simple circle. This design was inspired by the thought of two strangers from opposite sides of the world coming together to form a friendship.

Stitch

Eyelet Hole Stitch

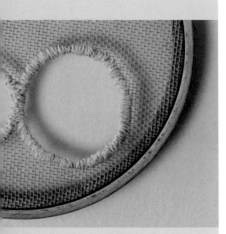

crewel screen art

Aluminum screening provides a stylish backdrop
for these simple circle motifs.

What You Need

3 pieces of aluminum screening, preferably old, with signs of wear, each 8 inches (20.3 x 20.3 cm) square

3 hoops, each 6 inches (15.2 cm) in diameter

Crewel wool thread, 2 skeins of medium pink, or any color of your choice

Chenille needle, size 22, or comparable crewel needle of choice

Permanent marker

Wire cutters

Scissors

Instructions

1 Lay one of the aluminum pieces on a flat surface.

2 Using the permanent marker, draw two circles, one small (approximately 1½ inches [3.8 cm] in diameter) and one big (approximately 2½ inches [6.3 cm] in diameter) on the piece of aluminum, using the picture on page 73 as a guide.

3 Using the wire cutters, cut the circles out.

4 Hoop the piece of screen just as you would a piece of fabric. Screw the hoop extra tight (see page 15).

5 Using the wire cutters, trim the excess screening as close as you can to the hoop.

6 Knot and thread the needle and embroider the screen using the Eyelet Hole Stitch.

7 Leave your finished work in the hoop and hang it on the wall.

8 Repeat steps 1-7 to complete the other hoops.

VARIATIONS

Try embroidering on other non-linen, non-fabric materials like handmade paper, plastic bags, cardboard, leather, vinyl, or felt. See how artistic you can be when you break the crewel rules!

I used Appleton crewel wool in color 943.

embroidered felt purse

Turn an everyday purse into a cool, contemporary clutch with this mod motif.

What You Need

Wool felted change purse in turquoise or a color of your choice

Crewel wool thread, 1 skein each of light yellow/orange, yellow/orange, and split pea yellow*, or colors of your choice

Chenille needle, size 24, or comparable crewel needle of choice

Fabric pen (the vanishing kind)

Scissors

Instructions

1 Using the fabric pen, draw a 16-point circle in the center of the felt purse, connecting each dot with a half-circle. You can also use the Sunflower diagram (see page 95). Print out the diagram, cut it out around the edge of the flower shape, and trace it onto the felt purse.

2 Starting with the Circular Filling Stitch, follow the instructions for the Sunflower design as shown on page 95. The felted wool is so thick that you won't need to use a hoop.

3 You're done!

VARIATION

Try this pattern on another felted wool item like a hat, bowl, or bag.

*I used Appleton crewel wool in colors 554, 555, and 997.

hooped crewel

Here's a cool crewel design tip: Leave your embroidered pieces in their hoops and hang them on the wall. Decorating has never been easier!

Pattern

China Blues 1, 2, 3, 5, 6 (see pages 88-93)

Stitches

Back Stitch, Broken Overcast Stitch, Circular Filling Stitch, French Knot, Overcast Stitch, Split Stitch, Straight Stitch

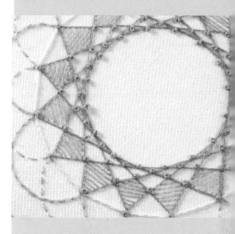

What You Need

5 pieces of white linen twill, each 9 inches square (23 x 23 cm)

5 wooden hoops, each 6 inches (15.25 cm) in diameter

Crewel wool, 1 skein each of deep kingfisher blue, light kingfisher blue, medium kingfisher blue, perfect sky blue, periwinkle blue, and pale kingfisher blue; 2 skeins each of kingfisher blue, medium sky blue, pale kingfisher blue, and split pea yellow*

Chenille needle, size 24, or comparable crewel needle of choice

Fabric pen (the vanishing kind)

Scissors

Sewing thread

Hand sewing needle

Instructions

1 Using the fabric pen, transfer one of the six China Blue patterns onto the center of a piece of the white linen fabric (see page 14).

2 Hoop the fabric, centering the design (see page 15).

3 Embroider the pattern, using colors and stitches as indicated in the China Blue diagram of your choice (see pages 88-93).

4 Block your finished crewelwork by spraying it with clean water. The piece should be completely wet. Then let the crewelwork dry flat, face up. Do not remove it from the hoop. (For more on blocking, see page 16.)

5 Turn your embroidery over while it's still in the hoop and trim the raw edge approximately 1 inch (2.5 cm) all the way around, leaving a 1-inch (2.5 cm) border.

6 Thread the hand sewing needle with 24 inches (60.9 cm) of a double thickness of the sewing thread.

7 With the hoop screw clasp at the top (12 o'clock) begin basting at 9 o'clock and continue clockwise, catching all of the fabric border until you get back to 9 o'clock. Gently pull the thread, gathering the fabric until it's fairly taut. Without letting the fabric get loose, insert the threaded needle at 3 o'clock and then at 9 o'clock again, going back and forth until the thread is too short and must be knotted (see page 17). These long stitches across the back of the crewelwork will allow you to hang the hoop on the wall like a picture.

8 Repeat steps 1-7 using the other China Blue patterns.

VARIATION

Try this project with other patterns from this book. You can alter the patterns and hoop sizes from 3 to 10 inches (7.6 to 25.4 cm). Why not cover a wall with a montage of your hooped crewelwork?

I used one skein each of Appleton crewel wool in colors 462, 482, 484, 485 and 563, and 2 skeins each in colors 481, 483, 562, and 997.

blossom sewing basket

Crewel embroidery makes this sewing basket extra special.
The bold stars and cheerful blossoms are easy embellishments.

Pattern

Delicate Doily (see page 94)
Marigold (see page 96)
Simple Daisy (see page 97)
Poppy (see page 97)
Twinkling Stars (see page 98)

Stitches

Straight Stitch, Split Stitch,
Spiderweb Stitch, French Knot

What You Need

Yellow plain-weave linen, 13 x 15 inches (33.1 x 38.1 cm)

White cotton fabric for lining, 13 x 15 inches (33.1 x 38.1 cm)

Hoop, 6 to 8 inches (15.2 to 20.3 cm) in diameter

Crewel wool thread, 1 skein each of light orange, light kingfisher blue, bright yellow, yellow/orange, and deep yellow/orange

Chenille needle, size 24, or comparable crewel needle of choice

Sewing basket with soft top, 7 x 9 inches (17.7 x 22.8 cm)

Tracing paper

Fabric pen or pencil

Scissors

Ruler

Sewing thread

Hand-sewing needle

Hot-glue gun

Instructions

1. Using the tracing paper and the fabric pen or pencil, randomly transfer several of the patterns listed above onto the yellow linen fabric (see page 14). You should end up with a border approximately 3 inches (7.6 cm) on all sides.

2. If your sewing basket top is not 7 x 9 inches (17.7 x 22.8 cm), cut your fabric 3 inches (7.6 cm) wider than your basket top on all sides. Then increase or decrease the number of flowers to fit your basket, making sure that some of the flowers run into the 3-inch (7.6 cm) border. Depending on the size of your basket, you may also need to enlarge or shrink the flowers. This project is based on a sewing basket with a 7 x 9-inch (17.7 x 22.8 cm) top. All of the flowers were shrunk a bit to fit.

3. Starting with the top left section of the design, hoop a portion of the fabric (see page 15). Because this design is much larger than the hoop, you will need to work in sections, unscrewing the hoop and rehooping as you complete an area.

④ Embroider the design, using the colors and stitches indicated in your selected patterns.

⑤ Block your finished crewelwork (see page 16).

⑥ Trim 1 inch (2.5 cm) from each side of your embroidery, leaving a 2-inch (5 cm) border on all sides. The linen fabric with finished crewelwork should now measure 11 x 13 inches (27.9 x 33 cm). Set aside.

⑦ Carefully remove the soft top from the existing sewing basket, including the cardboard backing. Usually these are glued into place. Remove the existing fabric.

⑧ Lay your crewelwork face down on a flat surface. Lay the foam insert from the sewing basket flat or hard side up on top of your crewelwork.

⑨ Using the sewing thread and the hand-sewing needle, make long stitches from one edge of the linen across to the opposite edge. Repeat, stitching both lengthwise and widthwise, until the crewelwork is securely "laced" to the foam insert.

⑩ Using the hot-glue gun, apply several lines of hot glue to the underside of the embroidered soft top and press it securely onto the sewing basket lid, crewel-side up. Now fill the basket with crewel notions and give it to a crewel crafter!

VARIATIONS

Choose other designs from this book for a different sewing basket look. Or try slightly overlapping the designs for a more intriguing and complicated final pattern.

I used Appleton crewel wool in colors Appleton 441, 482, 553, 555, and 557.

crewel pillow trio

The perfect accent pieces for any room, these impossible-to-ignore pillows will add style to your old sofa or easy chair. Grouped together, they have extra impact, but each one is sweet enough to stand on its own.

Pattern

Hollyhock (see page 96)
Delicate Doily (see page 94)
Zinnea (see page 100)

Stitches

Satin Stitch, Split Stitch, Straight Stitch, French Knot, Chain Stitch, Turkey Work Stitch

What You Need

To make the Hollyhock pillow cover:

White linen twill, 1 piece 18 inches square (45.7 x 45.7 cm) and 2 pieces 14 x 10 inches (35.5 x 25.4 cm)

Crewel wool thread, 1 skein each of light orange, bright orange/red, medium orange/red, and light kingfisher blue

To make the Delicate Doily pillow cover:

Turquoise linen plain weave, 1 piece 18 inches square (45.7 x 45.7 cm) and 2 pieces 14 x 10 inches (35.5 x 25.4 cm)

Crewel wool thread, 1 skein each of bright white and gray

Hoop, 6 inches (15.2 cm) in diameter

Chenille needle, size 24, or comparable crewel needle of choice

White cotton fabric for lining, 1 piece 14 inches square (35.5 x 35.5 cm) and 2 pieces 14 x 10 inches (35.5 x 25.4 cm)

Pillow form, 12 inches square (30.5 x 30.5 cm)

Tracing paper

Fabric pen or pencil

Scissors

Straight pins

Ruler

Sewing thread

Hand-sewing needle

Instructions

1 To make the red and orange pillow cover, transfer the Hollyhock pattern (page 14) onto the piece of white linen twill using the tracing paper and the fabric pen or pencil. To make the blue pillow cover, transfer the Delicate Doily pattern onto the center of the piece of turquoise linen fabric.

2 Hoop the fabric, centering the design (see page 15).

3 Embroider the design using colors and stitches as indicated in the Hollyhock or Delicate Doily diagram.

4 Block your finished crewelwork (see page 16).

5 Trim 2 inches (5 cm) from each side of your embroidery, leaving a 1-inch (2.5 cm) border on all sides. The linen fabric with the finished crewelwork should now measure 14 inches square (35.5 x 35.5 cm).

6 Lay your crewelwork face down on a flat surface. Lay the piece of 14-inch-square (35.5 x 35.5 cm) lining fabric on top of your crewelwork. Pin the two pieces of fabric together and baste with the sewing thread and hand sewing needle, using a series of long, 1- to 2-inch (2.5 to 5 cm) straight stitches in diagonal rows spaced about 3 inches (7.5 cm) apart. Don't make these stitches too tight, since you'll remove them later. Set aside.

The Motif Collection

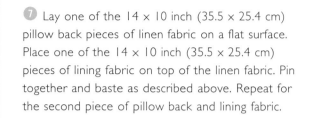

7 Lay one of the 14 x 10 inch (35.5 x 25.4 cm) pillow back pieces of linen fabric on a flat surface. Place one of the 14 x 10 inch (35.5 x 25.4 cm) pieces of lining fabric on top of the linen fabric. Pin together and baste as described above. Repeat for the second piece of pillow back and lining fabric.

8 For each pillow back piece, fold one long edge 1 inch (2.5 cm) in toward the lining. Press with a hot iron, or form a crease by rubbing your fingers along the fold. Fold again another 1 inch (2.5 cm), press or crease with your fingers, and pin along the folded edge .

9 Using the sewing thread, run a line of Blanket Stitch along the inside folded edge on each of the pieces. Remove the pins. You should now have two 14 x 8-inch (35.5 x 20.3 cm) pieces of basted, lined, and hemmed fabric that will be used to make the backing for your pillow.

10 Lay your basted and lined crewelwork face up on a flat surface. Lay one of the small pieces face down on top of the crewelwork with the fold in the middle and the left edges lining up. Pin the left edges together. Lay the other small piece in the same manner matched to the right side edge of the crewelwork, and pin the right side edges. The two folded and hemmed edges now overlap in the center.

11 Pin the top and bottom edges, and place a few pins through the center where the two smaller pieces overlap. Flip your work so that the lining side of the crewelwork is facing up.

12 Using the sewing thread and Back Stitch, stitch the three pieces together leaving a 1 inch (2.5 cm) seam allowance on all sides. Remove all of the pins.

13 Trim the seam allowances to ½ inch (1.3 cm).

14 Trim the corners, being careful not to cut too close to the stitching.

15 Remove the basting stitches.

16 Turn the pillow cover right side out.

17 Using the end of a blunt scissors, a knitting needle, or chopsticks, gently push out corners. Be careful not to push too hard or you'll poke a hole in your work.

18 Slip the pillow insert into the opening of your new pillow cover and adjust.

What You Need

To make the Zinnea pillow cover:

White linen twill, 1 piece 20 inches square (50.8 x 50.8 cm) and 2 pieces 16 x 12 inches (40.6 x 30.4 cm)

White cotton fabric for lining, 1 piece 16 inches square (40.6 x 40.6 cm) and 2 pieces 16 x 12 inches (40.6 x 30.4 cm)

Hoop, 6 to 10 inches (15.2 to 25.4 cm) in diameter

Crewel wool thread, 1 skein each of light orange, bright orange, bright orange/red, medium orange/red, deep orange/red, and kingfisher blue

Chenille needle, size 24, or comparable crewel needle of choice

Pillow form, 14 inches square (35.5 x 35.5 cm)

Tracing paper

Fabric pen or pencil

Scissors

Straight pins

Ruler

Sewing thread

Hand-sewing needle

Instructions

1 Using the tracing paper, the fabric pen or pencil, and the ruler, draw a 14-inch (35.5 cm) square in the center of the largest piece of white linen fabric. You should end up with a 3-inch (7.5 cm) border on all sides. This border will become your seam allowance.

2 Transfer the Zinnea pattern three times onto this marked fabric (see page 14). Two of the designs should overlap the square outline, falling into the seam allowance.

3 Hoop one of the designs (see page 15) and embroider it using the colors and stitches as indicated in the Zinnea diagram. Repeat for the other two designs.

4 Block your finished crewelwork (see page 16).

5 Trim 2 inches (5 cm) from each side of your embroidery, leaving a 1-inch (2.5 cm) border on all sides. The linen fabric with finished crewelwork should now measure 16 x 16 inches (40.6 x 40.6 cm).

6 Lay your crewelwork face down on a flat surface. Lay the large piece of lining fabric on top of your crewelwork. Pin the two pieces of fabric together and baste with the sewing thread and hand sewing needle, using a series of long, 1- to 2- inch (2.5 to 5 cm) straight stitches in diagonal rows spaced about 3 inches (7.5 cm) apart. Don't make these stitches too tight, since you'll remove them later. Set aside.

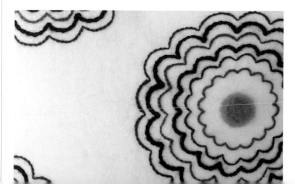

7 Lay one of the 16 × 12-inch (40.6 × 30.4 cm) pillow back pieces of white linen fabric on a flat surface. Place one of the 16 × 12-inch (40.6 × 30.4 cm) pieces of cotton lining fabric on top of the linen fabric. Pin together and baste as described above. Repeat for the second piece of pillow back and lining fabric.

8 For each pillow back piece, fold one long edge 1 inch (2.5 cm) in toward the lining. Press with a hot iron or form a crease by rubbing your fingers along the fold. Fold again another 1 inch (2.5 cm), press or crease with your fingers, and pin along the folded edge.

9 Using the sewing thread, run a line of Blanket Stitch along the inside folded edge on each of the pieces. Remove the pins. You should now have two 16 × 10-inch (40.6 × 25.4 cm) pieces of basted, lined, and hemmed fabric that will be used to make the backing for your pillow.

10 Lay your basted and lined crewelwork face up on a flat surface. Lay one of the small pieces face down on top of the crewelwork with the fold in the middle and the left edges lining up. Pin the left edges together. Lay the other small piece in the same manner matched to the right side edge of the crewelwork, and pin the right side edges. The two folded and hemmed edges should now overlap in the center.

⑪ Pin the top and bottom edges, and place a few pins through the center where the two smaller pieces overlap. Flip your work so that the lining side of the crewelwork is facing up.

⑫ Using the sewing thread and Back Stitch, stitch the three pieces together leaving a 1-inch (2.5 cm) hem on all sides. Remove all of the pins.

⑬ Trim the seam allowances to ½ inch (1.3 cm).

⑭ Trim the corners, being careful not to cut too close to the stitching.

⑮ Remove the basting stitches.

⑯ Turn the pillow right side out.

⑰ Using the end of a blunt scissors, a knitting needle, or chopsticks, gently push out corners. Be careful not to push too hard, or you'll poke a hole in your work.

⑱ Slip in the pillow form and adjust. Your pillow is done!

VARIATIONS

Change out the colors, perhaps using pinks or reds.

Increase or decrease the design size to fit any pillow.

Use a contrasting fabric for the back of the pillow.

I used Appleton crewel wool in colors 441, 442, 443, 445, 446, 482, 483, 991B, and 988.

china blue - 1

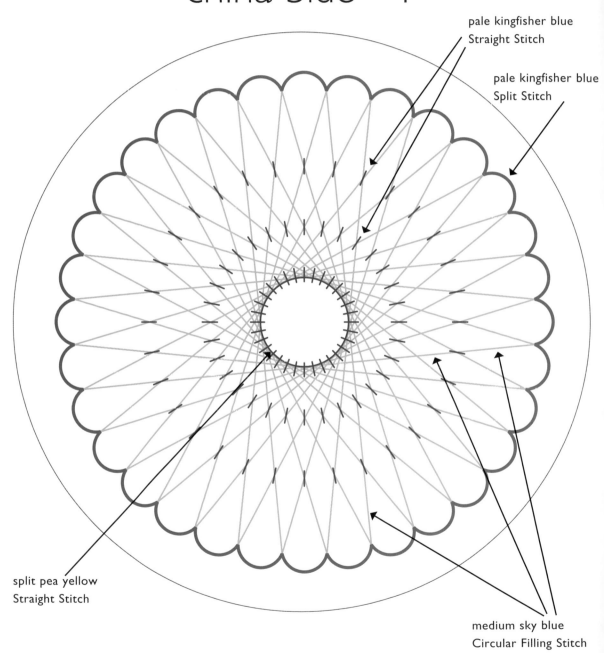

pale kingfisher blue
Straight Stitch

pale kingfisher blue
Split Stitch

split pea yellow
Straight Stitch

medium sky blue
Circular Filling Stitch

china blue - 2

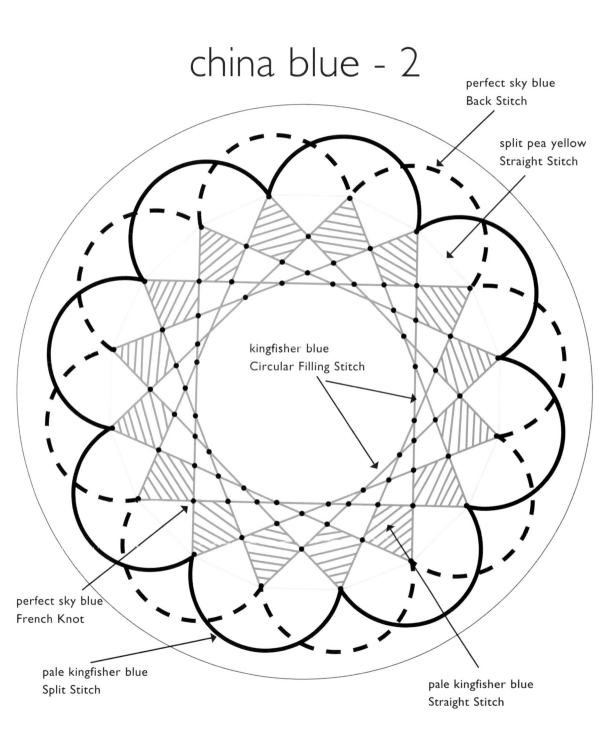

perfect sky blue
Back Stitch

split pea yellow
Straight Stitch

kingfisher blue
Circular Filling Stitch

perfect sky blue
French Knot

pale kingfisher blue
Split Stitch

pale kingfisher blue
Straight Stitch

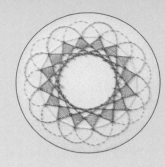

page 31

china blue - 3

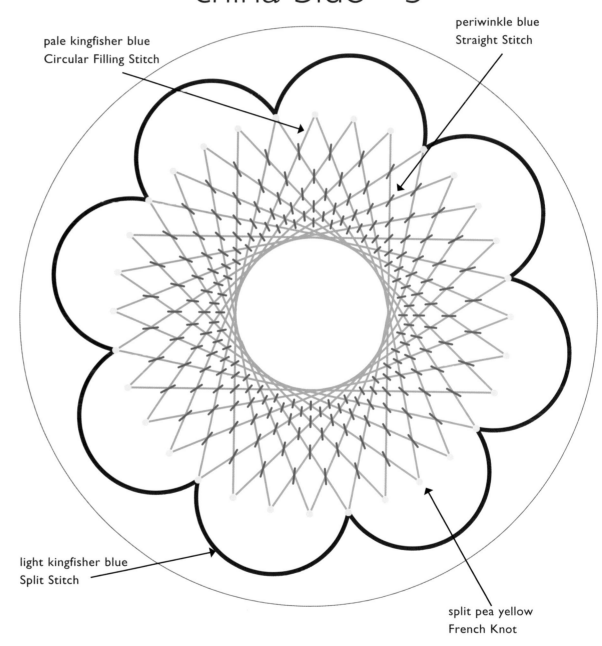

periwinkle blue
Straight Stitch

pale kingfisher blue
Circular Filling Stitch

light kingfisher blue
Split Stitch

split pea yellow
French Knot

china blue - 4

split pea yellow
Split Stitch

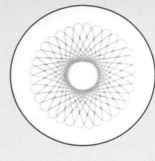

page 33

pale kingfisher blue
Circular Filling Stitch

split pea yellow
Straight Stitch

kingfisher blue
Straight Stitch

china blue - 5

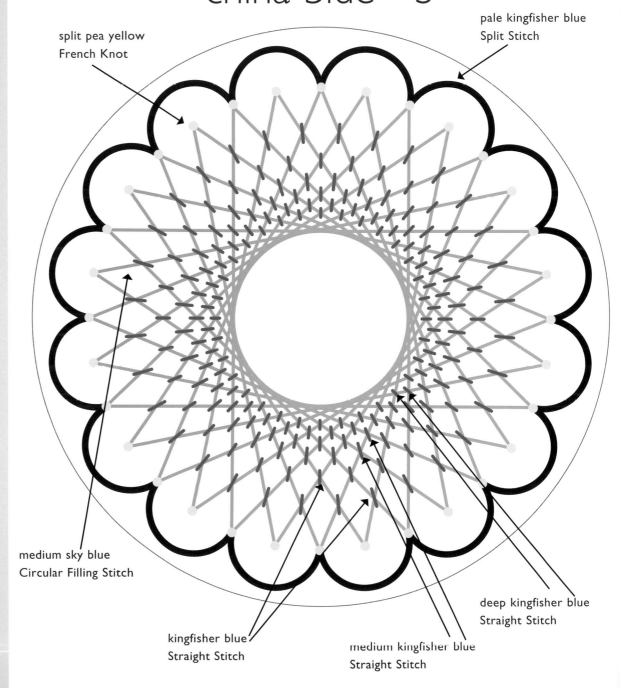

pale kingfisher blue
Split Stitch

split pea yellow
French Knot

medium sky blue
Circular Filling Stitch

deep kingfisher blue
Straight Stitch

kingfisher blue
Straight Stitch

medium kingfisher blue
Straight Stitch

china blue - 6

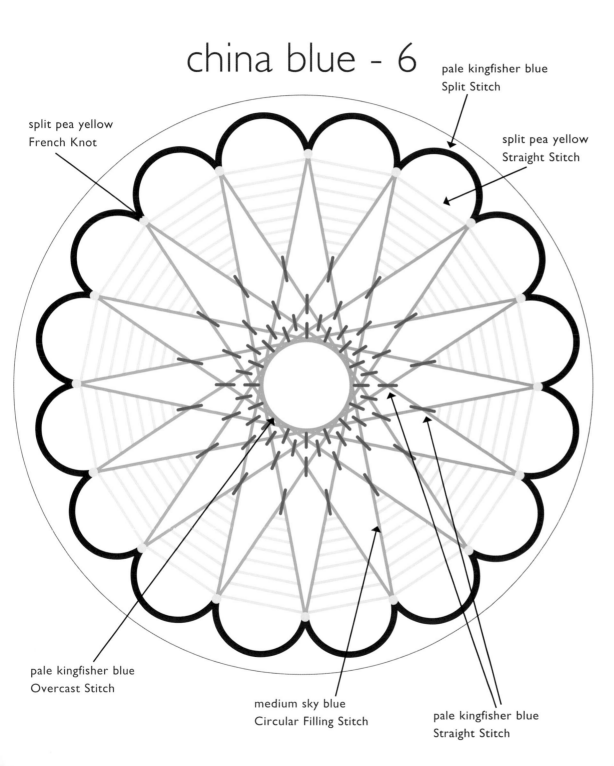

split pea yellow
French Knot

pale kingfisher blue
Split Stitch

split pea yellow
Straight Stitch

pale kingfisher blue
Overcast Stitch

medium sky blue
Circular Filling Stitch

pale kingfisher blue
Straight Stitch

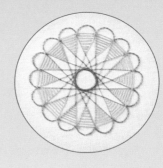

page 48

delicate doily

gray
Double Split Stitch

bright white
French Knot

gray
Straight Stitch

bright white
Straight Stitch

bright white
Double Split Stitch

sunflower

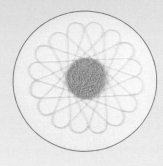

page 40

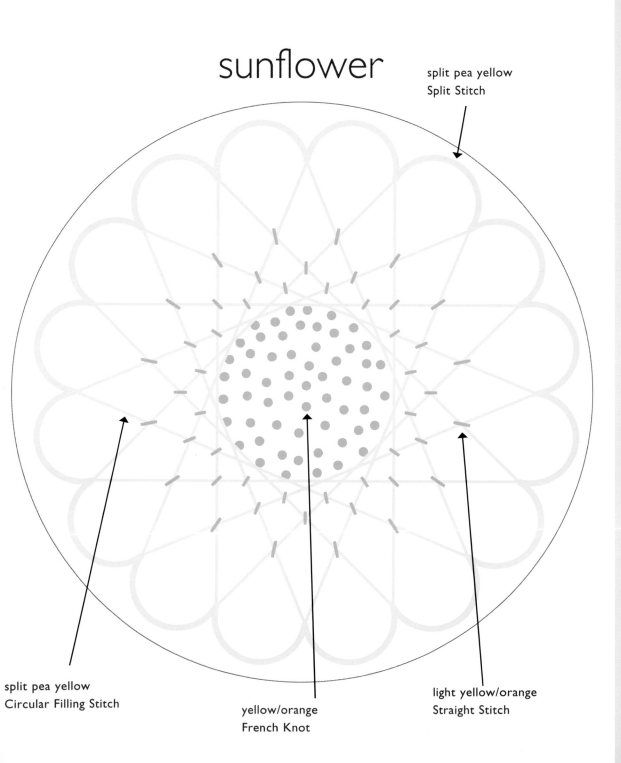

split pea yellow
Split Stitch

split pea yellow
Circular Filling Stitch

yellow/orange
French Knot

light yellow/orange
Straight Stitch

page 49

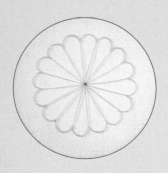

page 41

marigold

enlarge 200%

deep yellow/orange
French Knot

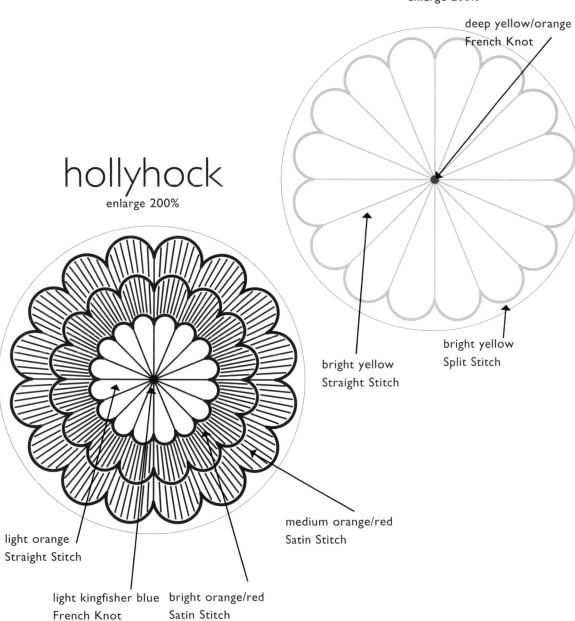

bright yellow
Straight Stitch

bright yellow
Split Stitch

hollyhock

enlarge 200%

light orange
Straight Stitch

light kingfisher blue
French Knot

bright orange/red
Satin Stitch

medium orange/red
Satin Stitch

simple daisy
enlarge 200%

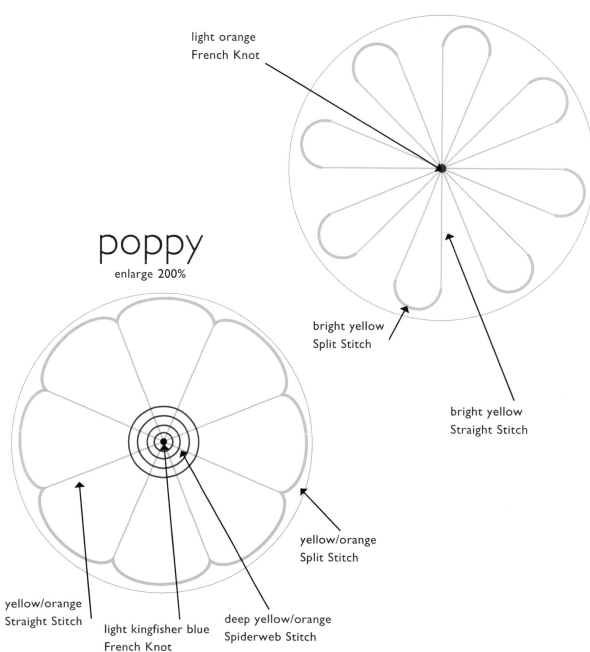

light orange
French Knot

bright yellow
Split Stitch

bright yellow
Straight Stitch

poppy
enlarge 200%

yellow/orange
Split Stitch

yellow/orange
Straight Stitch

light kingfisher blue
French Knot

deep yellow/orange
Spiderweb Stitch

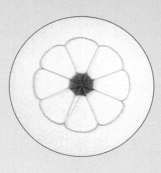

page 43

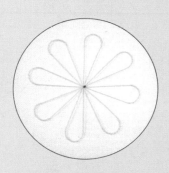

page 42

twinkling stars

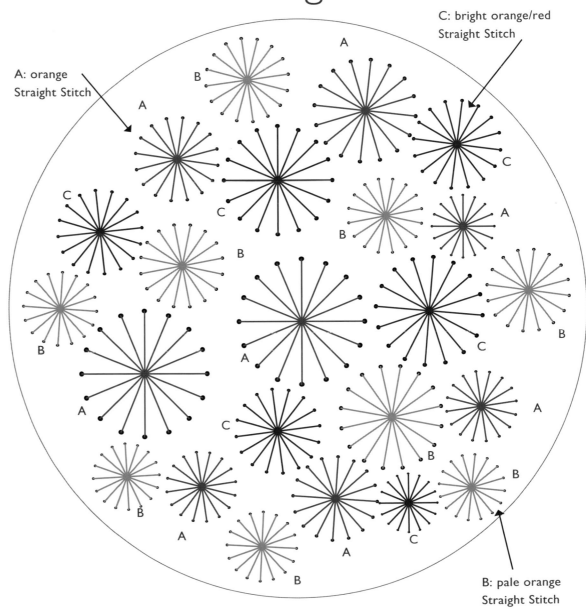

A: orange
Straight Stitch

C: bright orange/red
Straight Stitch

B: pale orange
Straight Stitch

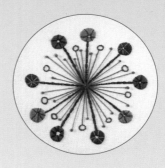

firecracker

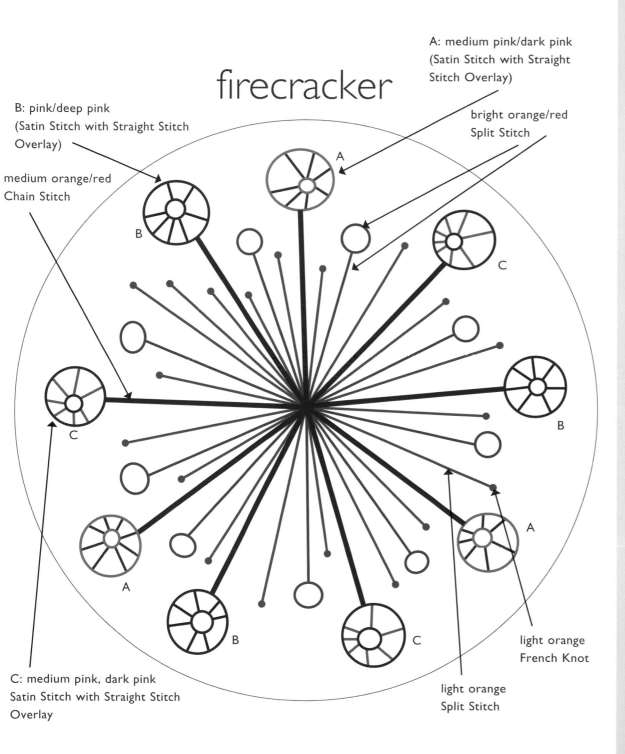

A: medium pink/dark pink
(Satin Stitch with Straight
Stitch Overlay)

bright orange/red
Split Stitch

B: pink/deep pink
(Satin Stitch with Straight Stitch
Overlay)

medium orange/red
Chain Stitch

light orange
French Knot

light orange
Split Stitch

C: medium pink, dark pink
Satin Stitch with Straight Stitch
Overlay

page 37

page 57

zinnea
enlarge 200%

medium orange/red
Chain Stitch

deep orange/red
Chain Stitch

kingfisher blue
Turkey Work

dahlia
enlarge 200%

yellow/orange
Split Stitch

bright yellow/orange
Split Stitch

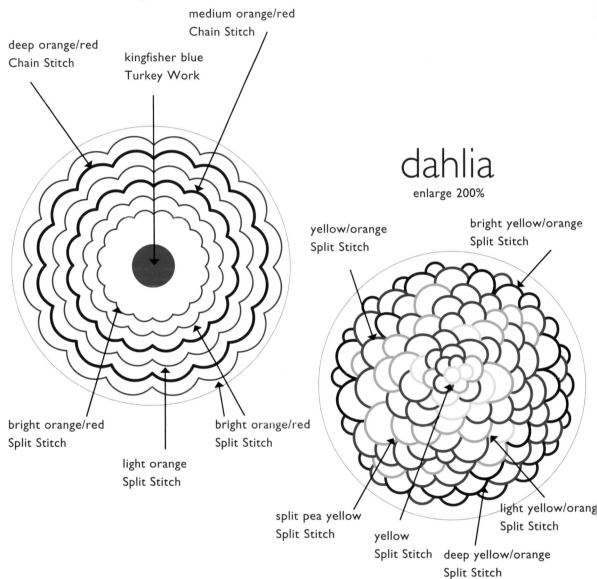

bright orange/red
Split Stitch

bright orange/red
Split Stitch

light orange
Split Stitch

split pea yellow
Split Stitch

yellow
Split Stitch

deep yellow/orange
Split Stitch

light yellow/orang
Split Stitch

crewel cilia

enlarge 200%

light kingfisher blue
Turkey Work

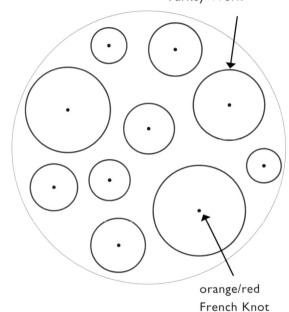

orange/red
French Knot

lazy daisy

enlarge 200%

split pea yellow
French Knot

pale yellow
French Knot

pale kingfisher blue
Back Stitch

yellow
French Knot

light kingfisher blue
Split Stitch

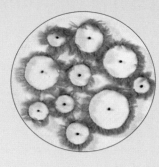

page 36

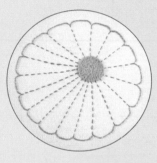

page 47

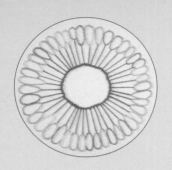

page 56

spring anemone

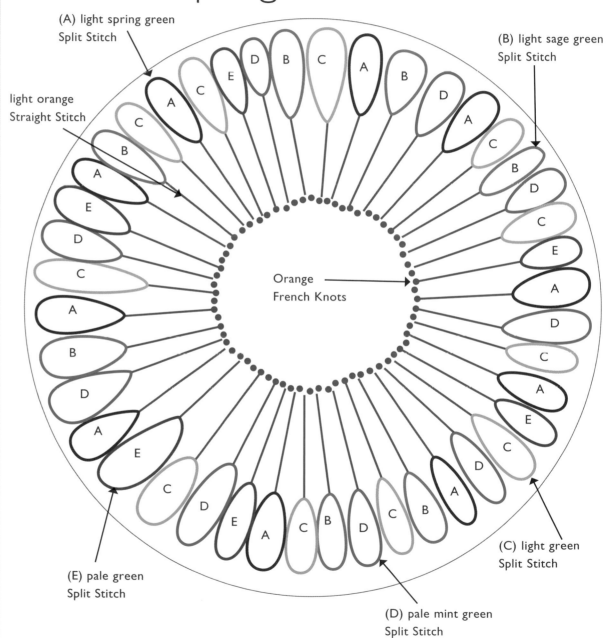

(A) light spring green
Split Stitch

(B) light sage green
Split Stitch

light orange
Straight Stitch

Orange
French Knots

(C) light green
Split Stitch

(E) pale green
Split Stitch

(D) pale mint green
Split Stitch

seed samples

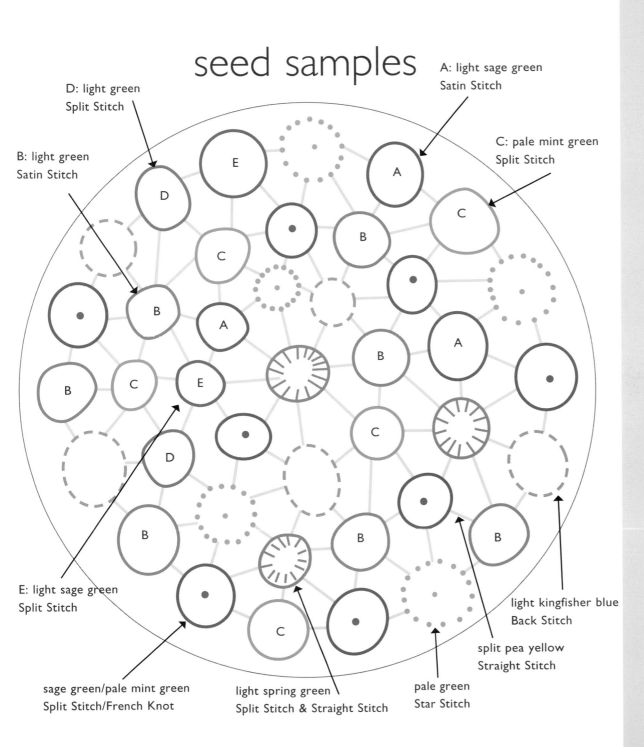

D: light green
Split Stitch

B: light green
Satin Stitch

A: light sage green
Satin Stitch

C: pale mint green
Split Stitch

E

D

A

C

B

C

B

B

A

C

E

B

A

B

A

B

D

C

B

B

C

E: light sage green
Split Stitch

sage green/pale mint green
Split Stitch/French Knot

light spring green
Split Stitch & Straight Stitch

pale green
Star Stitch

split pea yellow
Straight Stitch

light kingfisher blue
Back Stitch

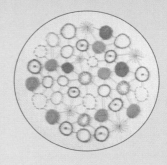

page 44

The Motif Collection

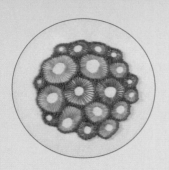

seed pod

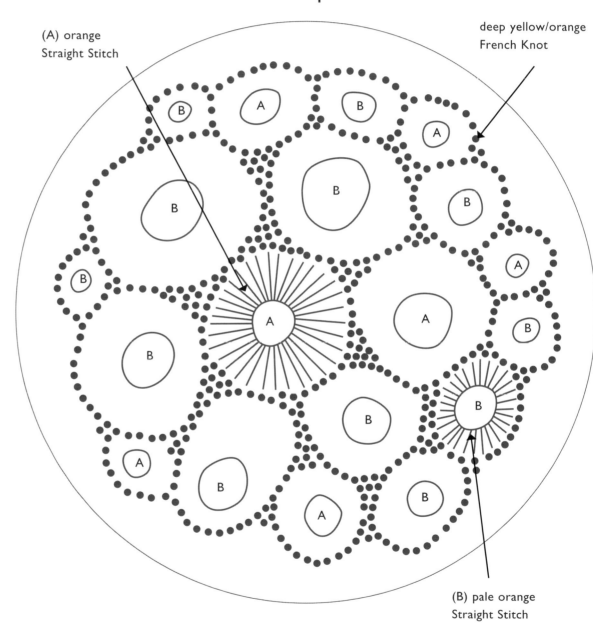

(A) orange
Straight Stitch

deep yellow/orange
French Knot

(B) pale orange
Straight Stitch

spiny spores

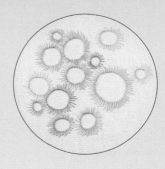

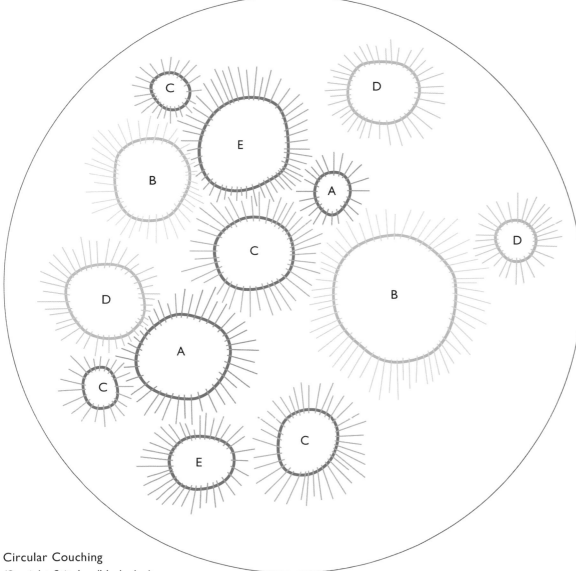

Circular Couching
(Straight Stitches/Underlay)
A- light sage green/pale mint green
B- light yellow/green/light green

C- light spring green/pale mint green
D- pastel green/light green

E- palest sage green/
pale mint green

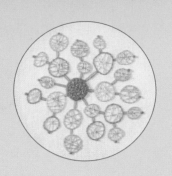

page 53

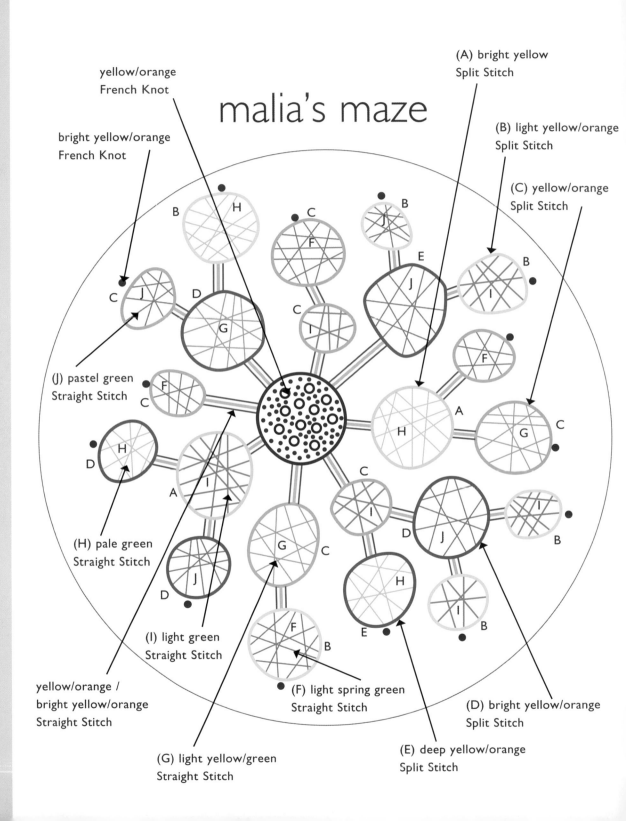

malia's maze

yellow/orange
French Knot

bright yellow/orange
French Knot

(A) bright yellow
Split Stitch

(B) light yellow/orange
Split Stitch

(C) yellow/orange
Split Stitch

(J) pastel green
Straight Stitch

(H) pale green
Straight Stitch

(I) light green
Straight Stitch

yellow/orange /
bright yellow/orange
Straight Stitch

(F) light spring green
Straight Stitch

(D) bright yellow/orange
Split Stitch

(E) deep yellow/orange
Split Stitch

(G) light yellow/green
Straight Stitch

sea anemone

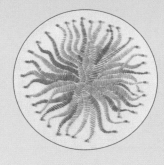

page 55

(A) orange
Straight Stitch

(B) pale orange
Straight Stitch

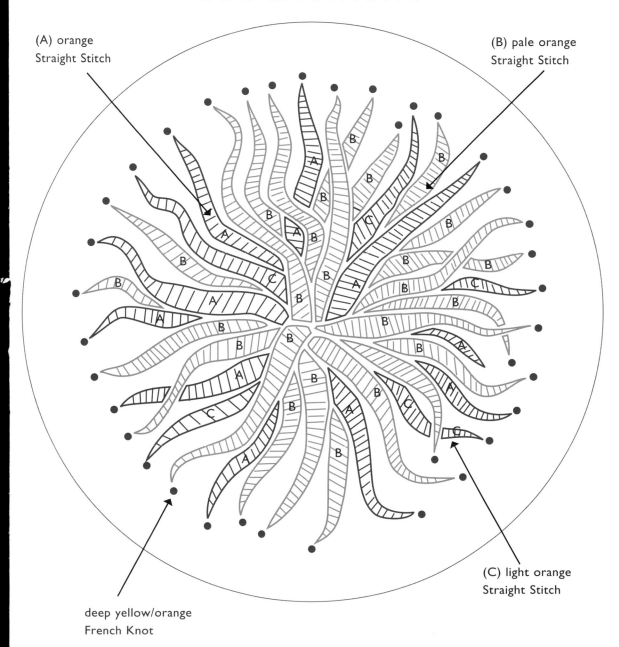

(C) light orange
Straight Stitch

deep yellow/orange
French Knot

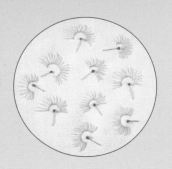

page 59

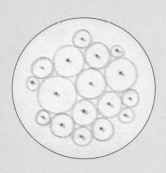

page 51

ella's wish
enlarge 200%

pale kingfisher blue
Straight Stitch

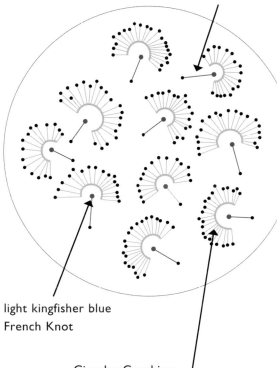

beaded bobbles
enlarge 200%

(A) light green Split Stitch
pale orange French Knot

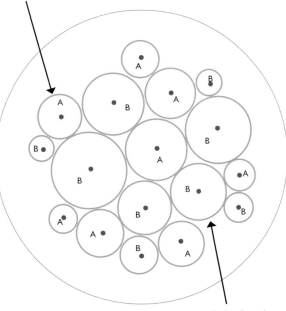

light kingfisher blue
French Knot

Circular Couching:
light spring green/gray
Straight stitches
light yellow/green
Underlay

(B) pale green Split Stitch
orange French Knot

cosmic burst

enlarge 200%

orange
Straight Stitch

pale orange
Straight Stitch

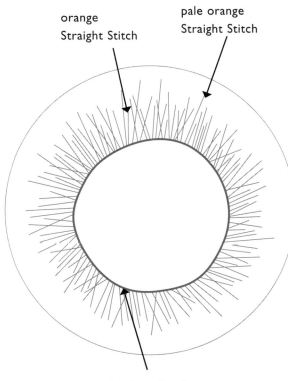

bright yellow/orange
Split Stitch

fiona's flower

enlarge 200%

pale kingfisher blue/ kingfisher blue
Split Stitch/French Knot

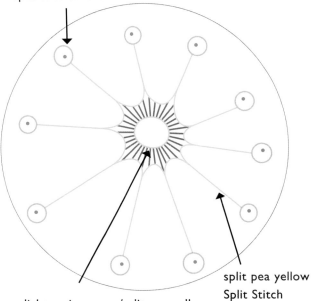

light spring green/split pea yellow
Satin Stitch with Split Stitch Outline

split pea yellow
Split Stitch

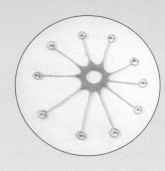

page 46

page 54

The Motif Collection

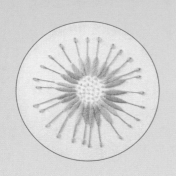

mirabella

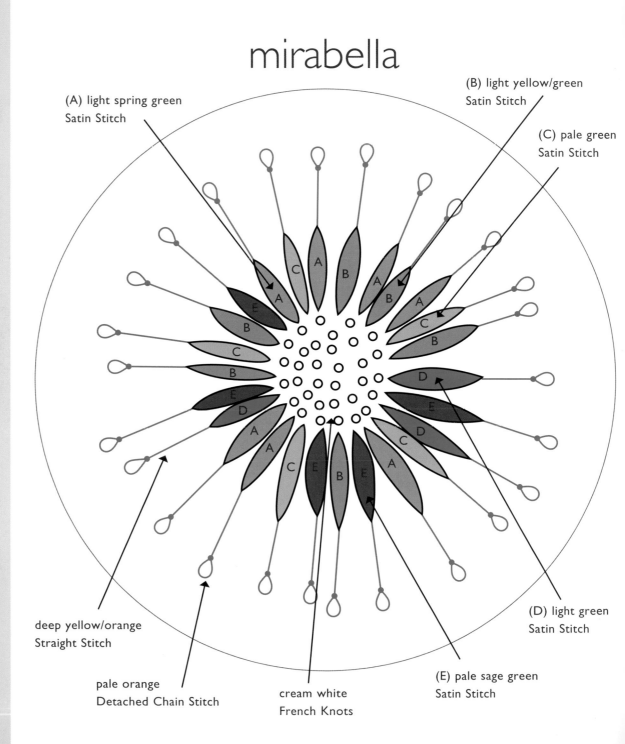

(A) light spring green
Satin Stitch

(B) light yellow/green
Satin Stitch

(C) pale green
Satin Stitch

(D) light green
Satin Stitch

(E) pale sage green
Satin Stitch

deep yellow/orange
Straight Stitch

pale orange
Detached Chain Stitch

cream white
French Knots

wyatt's rainbow

page 58

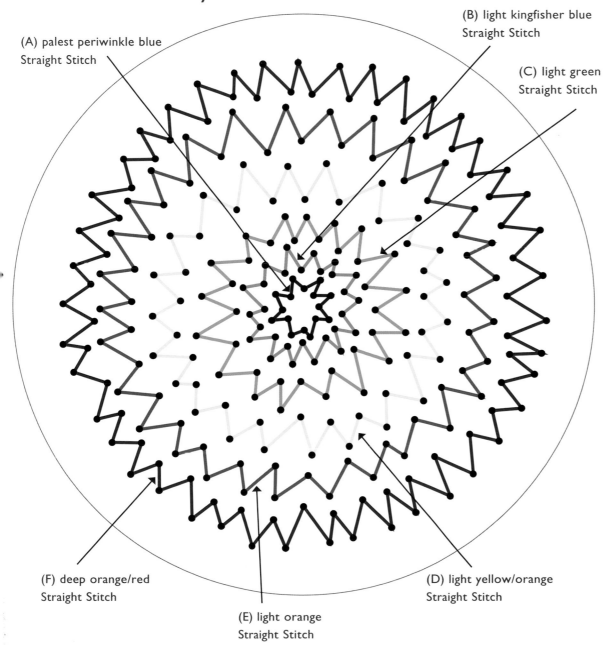

(A) palest periwinkle blue
Straight Stitch

(B) light kingfisher blue
Straight Stitch

(C) light green
Straight Stitch

(F) deep orange/red
Straight Stitch

(E) light orange
Straight Stitch

(D) light yellow/orange
Straight Stitch

about the author

As a young girl, Katherine Shaughnessy learned to sew on crewel kits given to her by her mother. The needle and thread have always figured into her artwork. Katherine holds a BFA from Miami University and an MFA from the School of the Art Institute of Chicago, where she focused on fiber arts. In 2003 she began developing contemporary designs for crewel embroidery kits, which she launched as the company Wool & Hoop. Her crewel kits are available at woolandhoop.com and at dozens of stores throughout the United States, Canada, Germany, and Japan. Katherine lives in Marfa, Texas, with her husband, Tom Michael, and their two children.

acknowledgments

Many thanks to my crafty mother, Joanne Shaughnessy, who introduced me to crewel embroidery when I was just five years old. I'm also indebted to my husband, Tom Michael, for his support and encouragement of my crewel endeavors. A special thanks goes to my children, Fiona Mae and Wyatt, whose everyday excitement for all things creative makes me oh-so-happy.

also from this author